GCSE

Mathematics

Higher

Revision Notes

Author
Peter Sherran

Series editor
Alan Brewerton

Letts

EDUCATIONAL

Every effort has been made to trace copyright holders and to obtain their permission for the use of copyright material. The authors and publishers will gladly receive information enabling them to rectify any error or omission in subsequent editions.

First published 1998

Letts Educational,
Schools and Colleges Division,
9–15 Aldine Street
London W12 8AW
Tel. 0181 740 2270
Fax: 0181 740 2280

Text © Peter Sherran 1998

Editorial, design and production by Hart McLeod, Cambridge

British Library Cataloguing-in-Publication Data
A CIP record for this book is available from the British Library

ISBN 1 84085 136 8

Printed and bound in Great Britain

Letts Educational is the trading name of BPP (Letts Educational) Ltd

Acknowledgements
The author and publisher are grateful to the staff at Cottenham Village College, Cambridge for their technical assistance.

Contents

Introduction

This book has been specifically designed to help you prepare for your GCSE exams in the easiest and most effective way. Keep this book with you throughout your revision – it is the key to your success.

How to use this book

All the information you need to know for your course is presented as a series of brief facts and explanations. These will help you understand and remember your work. Each page has a margin containing key tips from examiners showing you how to get extra marks or how to avoid common mistakes. There is also plenty of space in the margin for you to highlight key points, write your own notes and make references to other materials (class notes, textbooks, etc.). This will help you decide in which topics you feel confident or areas you do not fully understand. There is a short test at the end of each topic which will help test your understanding and boost your memory.

Preparing your revision programme

In most subjects you will have coursework, homework, revision, practice examination questions and a final examination. The examination may cause you the most anxiety. With proper preparation, however, you do not need to worry.

Make sure that you have allowed enough time to revise your work and make a list of all the things you have to do and your coursework deadlines.

Most important of all ... GOOD LUCK!

The examiner's report

Every year the examination boards publish reports on the previous year's examinations. The report shows areas in the examinations where students have performed well or badly and highlights mistakes that students frequently make. The examiners' reports can help you avoid making mistakes and therefore gain extra marks. **Recent examiners' reports highlight the following areas where students lost marks.**

- Premature rounding, truncation or a failure to give answers to the required degree of accuracy, loses marks unnecessarily and is often seen.

- Insufficient or careless working out.

- Lack of correct units, particularly in questions where units need to be stated.

- Vague answers with insufficient reference to the data when answering questions which ask you to 'Explain' or make comparisons.

- Poor skills in algebraic manipulation.

Common areas of difficulty

Some common areas of difficulty on Higher Level examination papers have occurred in the following topics:

- Using and interpreting indices *pages 9–10*

- Reverse percentage problems *page 18*

- Proportionality *pages 23–24*

- Interpretation and construction of graphs *pages 30–32*

- Transformations of graphs *page 33*

- Using the Trapezium rule to find the area under a graph *page 34*

- Graphs of inequalities *pages 39, 41*

- Angle properties of the circle *page 48*

- Further trigonometry including graphical representation *page 52*

- Vector geometry *page 56*

- Similarity *pages 60–61*

- Problems involving the Sine and Cosine rule *page 62*

- Frequency polygons *page 73*.

Number and algebra

Decimal places

Results obtained directly from measurement, or from calculation, often need to be rounded to a suitable degree of accuracy. This may be given by the number of figures to the right of the decimal point, i.e. the number of **decimal places**.

A calculator displays the value of $\sqrt{2}$ as shown below.

$$\boxed{1.414213562}$$

Working to two decimal places, for example, we see that $\sqrt{2}$ lies in between 1.41 and 1.42, that is $1.41 < \sqrt{2} < 1.42$. This situation may be represented on a number line.

$$\sqrt{2} = 1.414 \ldots$$

1.41	1.415	1.42

Since the figure in the *third* decimal place is **less than 5**, it follows that $\sqrt{2}$ is closer to 1.41 and so its value is **rounded down**. This is written as

$$\sqrt{2} = 1.41 \text{ correct to 2 d.p.}$$

However, in a value such as $10\pi = 31.4159 \ldots$, where the figure in the third decimal place is equal to **5 or more**, we **round up** to obtain $10\pi = 31.42$ correct to 2 d.p.

The same basic process applies when rounding to a different degree of accuracy.

Significant figures

The most significant figure in any number is the non-zero figure with the highest place value.

When rounding a value to a given number of significant figures, care must be taken to maintain the place value of the figures that remain.

Examples

Value	to 3 s.f.	to 2 s.f.	to 1 s.f.
4.207	4.21	4.2	4
1349	1350	1300	1000
0.003 604	0.003 60	0.0036	0.004

This zero counts as a significant figure.

6

Directed numbers

Positive and negative numbers are known collectively as **directed numbers** since a change of sign is often associated with a change of direction.

A number line provides a convenient way of representing directed numbers, which lie in order along its length, increasing in size from left to right.

Negative direction ◄───► Positive direction

```
 -5      -4      -3      -2      -1       0       1       2       3       4       5
 |       |       |       |       |       |       |       |       |       |       |
```

Addition and subtraction

The operations of addition and subtraction may be represented as movements, along the number line, to the right and to the left respectively.

The symbol used for the operation of subtraction is also used to indicate that a number has a negative sign. Care is needed to distinguish between these uses, particularly when using a calculator. A number without a negative sign is positive.

Examples

$2 - 5 = -3$ Start at 2 and move to the left 5 places to finish at -3.

$-4 + 3 = -1$ Start at -4 and move to the right 3 places to finish at -1.

When the number to be added (or subtracted) is negative, the normal direction of movement is reversed.

Examples

$-3 - (-2)$ is the same as $-3 + 2 = -1$.

$-1 + (-4)$ is the same as $-1 - 4 = -5$.

> The negative sign changes the operation:
> $- (-)$ becomes $+$,
> and $+ (-)$ becomes $-$.

Multiplication and division

Multiplying or dividing some value by a positive number leaves its sign unchanged, but multiplying or dividing by a negative number reverses the sign.

Examples

$$3 \times 2 = 6 \quad 3 \times -2 = -6 \quad -3 \times 2 = -6 \quad -3 \times -2 = 6.$$
$$12 \div 3 = 4 \quad 12 \div -3 = -4 \quad -12 \div 3 = -4 \quad -12 \div -3 = 4.$$

Using a calculator

Most scientific or graphic calculators have a special $\boxed{+/-}$ or $\boxed{(-)}$ key for entering negative numbers and will often give the wrong answers if the subtract key alone is used.

For example, $3 - (-5)$ should be keyed in as

$\boxed{3}\ \boxed{-}\ \boxed{5}\ \boxed{+/-}$ or $\boxed{3}\ \boxed{-}\ \boxed{(-)}\ \boxed{5}$

to give 8 as the answer (since $3 - (-5) = 3 + 5 = 8$).

Completing the number system

The number line

The number line may be used for calculations with directed numbers, as previously seen, but the link between points on the line and the number system is more fundamental.

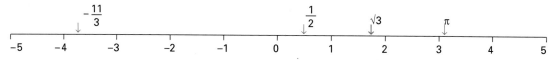

Every number has a unique position on the number line and, conversely, every point on the number line corresponds to a unique number.

The pattern of values labelled below the number line may be continued indefinitely in both directions . . . −5, −4, −3, −2, −1, 0, 1, 2, 3, 4, 5, . . . to produce the set of numbers known as the **integers**.

The integers alone clearly leave gaps on the number line that must be occupied by numbers of a different form, i.e. **non-integral** values.

Rational numbers

Any number that can be expressed exactly as a ratio $\frac{a}{b}$ of two integers ($b \neq 0$) is said to be a **rational number**. It follows that every integer n is itself a rational number since, for example, n may be expressed as $\frac{n}{1}$.

Every *terminating* decimal, i.e. every decimal with a finite number of decimal places, is rational. Some examples are

$$0.7 = \frac{7}{10} \text{ and } -3.142 = \frac{-3142}{1000}.$$

Every *recurring* decimal is a rational number.

For example, let $x = 0.\overset{\bullet\bullet}{32}$

$$= 0.3232323232 \ldots$$

then $100x = 32.3232323232 \ldots$ and subtracting gives

$$99x = 32$$

i.e. $x = \frac{32}{99}$.

Every numerical value found by your calculator is a rational number.

The rational numbers are clearly very important but, despite their abundance, they do not account for all of the points on the number line.

Irrational numbers

Any number that is a non-terminating decimal without a repeating pattern cannot be expressed *exactly* as the ratio of two integers and is said to be **irrational**.

The rational numbers and the irrational numbers, together, completely fill the number line; every number is either rational or irrational.

One example of an irrational number is π. It is impossible to write down the exact value of π even though it has been worked out to millions of decimal places. In practice, we use rational numbers such as $\frac{22}{7}$ or 3.142 as *approximations* to π in calculations.

Square roots provide a rich source of irrational numbers. For example, the square root of any positive integer is either itself an integer or irrational.

Examples

$\sqrt{2}$ and $\sqrt{3}$ are irrational, but $\sqrt{9} = 3$ which is an integer and is therefore rational.

Be careful though, because the square roots of some non-integer values can be found exactly. For example, $\sqrt{6.25} = 2.5$ which is rational.

Irrational numbers are far more common than might be supposed since, for example, combining any non-zero rational number with any irrational number under addition, subtraction, multiplication or division will always produce an irrational number.

Examples

$1 + \sqrt{5}$, $\frac{\sqrt{3}}{2}$, 4π and $\pi - 2$ are all irrational.

In the same way, pairs of rational numbers always combine to produce rational numbers. However, when combining pairs of irrational numbers the situation is not straightforward. Generally, the result will be irrational but examples can be constructed to give rational answers.

Examples

$\sqrt{2} + \sqrt{3}$ is irrational, but adding $(5 + \sqrt{2})$ and $(3 - \sqrt{2})$ gives 8 which is rational.

$\sqrt{2}\,\pi$ is irrational, but $5\sqrt{2} \times \sqrt{2} = 5 \times (\sqrt{2} \times \sqrt{2}) = 5 \times 2 = 10$ which is rational.

It is always possible to find an irrational number that lies in a given range. For example, to find an irrational number between 31 and 32 you could take an irrational number that you are familiar with, such as π, and adjust it. In this case, both $(\pi + 28)$ and 10π satisfy the given condition.

Exam questions on this topic often involve recognising rational and irrational numbers or constructing irrational numbers that satisfy given conditions.

Index notation

An expression such as $a \times a \times a \times a$ may be written in a shorter way as a^4 which is read as 'a to the **power** of 4'. The letter a is regarded as the **base** of the expression.

Starting from $a^4 = a \times a \times a \times a$ and dividing both sides by a gives

$$\frac{a^4}{a} = \frac{a \times a \times a \times a}{a} = a^3$$

Continuing to divide successively by a produces a sequence of results:

$$a^2 = a \times a$$
$$a^1 = a$$
$$a^0 = 1$$
$$a^{-1} = \frac{1}{a}$$
$$a^{-2} = \frac{1}{a^2}$$

provided $a \neq 0$

$\frac{1}{a}$ is known as the **reciprocal** of a.

The reciprocal of $\frac{a}{b}$ is $\frac{b}{a}$.

Some further general results are suggested by considering simple cases.

$$a^2 \times a^3 = (a \times a) \times (a \times a \times a) = a^5$$

$$a^6 \div a^2 = \frac{a \times a \times a \times a \times a \times a}{a \times a} = a^4$$

Powers of the same base are added when multiplying and subtracted when dividing.

$$\left(a^2\right)^3 = a^2 \times a^2 \times a^2 = a^6 \left(= a^{2 \times 3}\right)$$

When raising a base to two successive powers, the powers must be multiplied.

$$\left(a^{\frac{1}{2}}\right)^2 = a^1 = a \text{ thus } a^{\frac{1}{2}} = \sqrt{a}$$

Roots may also be expressed as reciprocal powers.

$$a^{\frac{3}{2}} = \left(a^{\frac{1}{2}}\right)^3 = (\sqrt{a})^3; \text{ alternatively,}$$

$$a^{\frac{3}{2}} = \left(a^3\right)^{\frac{1}{2}} = \sqrt{a^3}$$

Fractional powers of a given base may need to be found in two stages. These stages may be taken in either order.

The rules of indices

An alternative name for the power of a number is its **index** and so the rules for working with powers are sometimes called the **rules of indices**.

These rules are not given on the formulae sheet in the examination and so they must be learned.

$$a^m \times a^n = a^{m+n} \qquad \frac{a^m}{a^n} = a^m \div a^n = a^{m-n} \qquad \left(a^m\right)^n = a^{mn}$$

$$a^{-n} = \frac{1}{a^n} \qquad a^{\frac{1}{n}} = \sqrt[n]{a} \qquad a^{\frac{m}{n}} = \sqrt[n]{a^m} = (\sqrt[n]{a})^m$$

Calculator techniques for finding powers and roots are given on page 19.

Examples

$$8^{\frac{2}{3}} = (\sqrt[3]{8})^2 = 2^2 = 4$$

$$\sqrt{5} \times 5^{\frac{3}{2}} = 5^{\frac{1}{2}} \times 5^{\frac{3}{2}} = 5^2 = 25$$

Standard form

A number in standard form is written as $A \times 10^n$ where $1 \le A < 10$ and n is an integer. This simplifies the way that very large or very small numbers are written.

Example

A light-year is the distance that light travels in a year and is approximately 5 878 000 000 000 miles. The two most important features of this number are the figures 5 878, and its order of magnitude given by their place values. In standard form this would be written as

$$5.878 \times 10^{12} \text{ miles}$$

5 878 000 000 000
12 places

A decimal point is included to make this part lie between 1 and 10.

This part restores the place values of the figures to their original level.

To express very small numbers in standard form the value of n must be negative.

Example

The diameter of a hydrogen atom is approximately 0.000 000 01 cm. In standard form this would be written as

8 places

$$1 \times 10^{-8} \text{ cm}$$

This should be left as 1 rather than 1.0 because the information is only given correct to 1 s.f. Using 1.0 suggests accuracy to 2 s.f.

Multiplying by 10^{-8} reduces the place value of the 1 to its original level.

Numbers in standard form may be entered directly into a calculator using the EXP key (or EE key) which simplifies the key sequence needed.

Examples

3.7×10^{11} is keyed in as 3.7 EXP 11.

It is important to use the *exact* key sequence.

To calculate the value of $p = \dfrac{3.7 \times 10^{11}}{8.1 \times 10^{-7}}$ the key sequence becomes

3.7 EXP 11 ÷ 8.1 EXP 7 +/− =

giving

You may need to enter this as (−) 7.

$p = 4.6 \times 10^{17}$ (correct to 2 s.f.)

Take a note of how *your* calculator displays standard form. Most calculators do not show the information in the way that it is *written*, so you are likely to **lose marks** if you simply copy the display when required to give answers in standard form.

Questions

1 (a) Round 2.976 to 2 d.p.

   (b) Round 4387.2 to 1 s.f.

2 Complete the following without using a calculator:

   (a) $-3 + 5 =$ __   (b) $-2 - 4 =$ __   (c) $-6 \times 5 =$ __

   (d) $-12 \div -3 =$ __   (e) $5 +$ __ $= -3$ (f) __ $- -5 = -5$

3 Use a calculator to work out $17.3 \div -8$.

4 Which of the following are irrational?

   $3.142, \quad \pi, \quad \sqrt{3}, \quad \sqrt{7} \times 2\sqrt{7}, \quad \sqrt{1.21}, \quad (\sqrt{5} - 1), \quad (\sqrt{5} - 1)^2, \quad (\sqrt{5} + 1)(\sqrt{5} - 1)$

5 Express $0.2\overset{\bullet}{1}\overset{\bullet}{7}$ in the form $\dfrac{a}{b}$, where a and b are integers.

6 Simplify:

   (a) $(a^3)^2$ (b) $\dfrac{b^2 \times b^3}{b^6}$

7 Find the value of n such that $\dfrac{t^2}{\sqrt{t}} = \sqrt{t^n}$.

8 Write these in standard form.

   (a) 461 000 000   (b) 0.000 072

9 Write these as ordinary numbers.

   (a) 3.63×10^5 (b) 9.6×10^{-6}

10 Use a calculator to find the value of $\dfrac{8.63 \times 10^{11}}{3.9 \times 10^{-4}}$ in standard form correct to 3 s.f.

Relationships between numbers and computation methods
Multiples and factors

Multiples

Examiner's tips and your notes

The **multiples** of a whole number are produced by multiplying it by other whole-number values. Every whole number is a multiple of itself.

Example

The first five multiples of 8 are   8, 16, ⟨24⟩, 32 and 40.

Similarly, the first five multiples of 12 are   12, ⟨24⟩, 36, 48 and 60.

24 is the smallest number that is both a multiple of 8 and a multiple of 12. We say that 24 is the **lowest common multiple** (LCM) of 8 and 12.

Factors

The **factors** of a whole number are whole-number values that divide into it without leaving any remainder. Every whole number is a factor of itself.

Example

The factors of 24 are   1, 2, 3, 4, 6, ⟨8⟩, 12 and 24.

The factors of 32 are   1, 2, 4, ⟨8⟩, 16 and 32.

The largest number that is a factor of both numbers is 8. We say that 8 is the **highest common factor** (HCF) of 24 and 32.

The factors occur in pairs:

1, 2, 3, 4, 6, 8, 12, 24

Each factor less than $\sqrt{24}$ is paired with a factor greater than $\sqrt{24}$.

Prime numbers

You are expected to know the prime numbers up to 59 and may be required to recognise them, within a list of numbers, in the exam.

A **prime number** is a whole number with exactly two distinct factors. It follows that 1 is not a prime number since it only has itself as a factor.

The smallest prime number is 2, which is also the only even prime number.

The prime numbers less than 100 are 2, 3, 5, 7, 11, 13, 17, 19, 23, 29, 31, 37, 41, 43, 47, 53, 59, 61, 67, 71, 73, 79, 83, 89 and 97.

The factors of 24 include 2 and 3 which are prime numbers, and so are referred to as the **prime factors** of 24.

Composite numbers

A **composite** number is a number with at least three factors. No prime numbers are included and the smallest composite number is 4.

Any composite number can be expressed as a product of its prime factors. For example, $24 = 2 \times 2 \times 2 \times 3$ which may be written as $2^3 \times 3$ using **index notation**.

A simple way to convert a number into the product of its prime factors is to use a **factor tree**. A factor tree can often be constructed in more than one way, but the end result is always the same, i.e. the prime factorisation of a number is unique.

Example

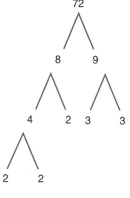

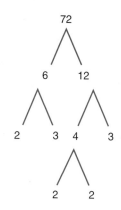

$72 = 2 \times 2 \times 2 \times 3 \times 3$

$\quad\quad = 2^3 \times 3^2$

$72 = 2 \times 3 \times 2 \times 2 \times 3$

$\quad\quad = 2^3 \times 3^2$

Prime factors may be used to find the LCM or the HCF of some numbers.

Example

Find the HCF and the LCM of 2160 and 2700.

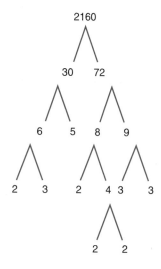

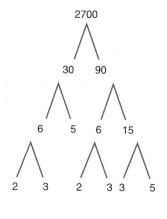

$2160 = 2^4 \times 3^3 \times 5$

$2700 = 2^2 \times 3^3 \times 5^2$

Each number contains factors of 2^2, 3^3 and 5. The HCF may now be found by multiplying these together to give $2^2 \times 3^3 \times 5 = 540$.

The LCM must contain the highest power of each prime number represented in either number, i.e. 2^4, 3^3 and 5^2 giving $2^4 \times 3^3 \times 5^2 = 10\ 800$.

Fractions

In a fraction of the form $\dfrac{a}{b}$, a is called the **numerator** and b is called the **denominator**. For **proper** fractions, $a < b$; for **improper** fractions, $a > b$.

Improper fractions may be written as **mixed numbers** containing a mixture of a whole number and a proper fraction, e.g. $\frac{9}{4} = 2\frac{1}{4}$.

Given any fraction, an **equivalent** one may be produced by multiplying (or dividing) the numerator and denominator by the same number.

Examples

$$\frac{2}{3} \overset{\times 5}{=} \frac{10}{15} \quad \text{and} \quad \frac{24}{32} \overset{\div 8}{=} \frac{3}{4}.$$

The fraction $\frac{24}{32}$ **cancels** to $\frac{3}{4}$ which represents the fraction in its **lowest terms**.

Similarly, in algebra $\frac{x + \frac{1}{2}}{x - \frac{1}{2}} = \frac{2x + 1}{2x - 1}$.

Addition and subtraction

The addition and subtraction of fractions which have the same denominator is much the same as the addition and subtraction of 'like terms' in algebra. For example, just as $2x + 3x = 5x$ we can regard $\frac{2}{7} + \frac{3}{7}$ as $2(\frac{1}{7}) + 3(\frac{1}{7}) = 5(\frac{1}{7}) = \frac{5}{7}$.

Fractions that do not have the same denominator may be added and subtracted by using equivalent fractions in which the denominators are the same.

Examples

(a) $\frac{7}{8} - \frac{5}{12} = \frac{21}{24} - \frac{10}{24} = \frac{11}{24}$

(b) $\frac{x}{3} + \frac{x}{2} = \frac{2x}{6} + \frac{3x}{6} = \frac{5x}{6}$

Multiplication and division

In general,

$$\frac{a}{b} \times \frac{c}{d} = \frac{ac}{bd}$$

However, it is usually simpler to cancel any factors common to the top and bottom rows first. Mixed numbers may be multiplied in this way by writing them as improper fractions.

Dividing by any number is equivalent to multiplying by its reciprocal. For example, dividing by 2 is the same as multiplying by $\frac{1}{2}$. In general,

$$\frac{a}{b} \div \frac{c}{d} = \frac{a}{b} \times \frac{d}{c}$$

Examples

(a) $\frac{\overset{1}{\cancel{8}}}{\cancel{9}_3} \times \frac{\overset{5}{\cancel{15}}}{\cancel{16}_2} = \frac{5}{6}$

(b) $10\frac{1}{2} \div 2\frac{1}{3} = \frac{21}{2} \div \frac{7}{3} = \frac{\overset{3}{\cancel{21}}}{2} \times \frac{3}{\cancel{7}_1} = \frac{9}{2} = 4\frac{1}{2}$

The idea that fractions may be expressed in equivalent forms is one of the most useful when solving problems in which they are involved.

Most scientific calculators allow fraction calculations to be entered directly using the $\boxed{a^b/c}$ key.

However, make sure that, in the exam, you show sufficient working to make your method clear.

Percentages

'Per cent' means 'per hundred', and so n% means n parts per hundred or $\frac{n}{100}$.

To calculate a percentage of some amount, convert the percentage to an equivalent form as a fraction or decimal and multiply.

Questions involving percentages appear on exam papers every year and so it is important to be aware of the various techniques required.

Examples

(a) 25% of 32

$= \frac{1}{4}$ of 32 (i.e. 32 ÷ 4)

$= 8$

(b) 7.8% of 425

$= \frac{7.8}{100} \times 425$

$= 0.078 \times 425$

$= 33.15$

Some percentage calculations may be worked out simply using fractions. For example, you should recognise that

$50\% = \frac{1}{2}$, $25\% = \frac{1}{4}$,

$12\frac{1}{2}\% = \frac{1}{8}$ and $33\frac{1}{3}\% = \frac{1}{3}$.

It also follows, for example, that $66\frac{2}{3}\% = \frac{2}{3}$.

Further applications of these techniques will be found on pages 25-6.

Reducing by a percentage

There are two basic approaches to reducing some amount by a percentage and both need to be understood.

Example

A pair of trainers originally priced at £39.99 are to be reduced by 15% in a sale. Find the sale price (to the nearest penny).

Method A

15% of £39.99 $= \frac{15}{100} \times £39.99$

$= 0.15 \times £39.99$

$= £5.9985 = £6.00$ (to the nearest penny)

Sale price = £33.99 (to the nearest penny).

In method A, the actual reduction is calculated first and then subtracted from the original amount.

Method B: the scale factor method

100% − 15% = 85%

85% of £39.99 $= \frac{85}{100} \times £39.99$

$= 0.85 \times £39.99$

$= £33.9915 = £33.99$ (to the nearest penny)

Sale price = £33.99 (to the nearest penny).

In method B, the original amount is represented by 100%. When 15% is subtracted, 85% of it remains.

Multiplying by the scale factor 0.85 has the required **reducing** effect on the original amount.

Increasing by a percentage

Once again, there are two basic approaches and both need to be learned.

Example

A property worth £75 000 a year ago has increased in value by 3%. What is its current value?

Method A

$$3\% \text{ of } £75\,000 = \frac{3}{100} \times £75\,000$$

$$= 0.03 \times £75\,000$$

Increase $\quad\quad\quad = £2250$

Current value $\quad - £75\,000 + £2250$

$$= £77\,250$$

The actual increase may be calculated first, in the usual way. It is then added to the original amount.

Method B: the scale factor method

$$100\% + 3\% = 103\%$$

$$103\% \text{ of } £75\,000 = \frac{103}{100} \times £75\,000$$

$$= 1.03 \times £75\,000$$

$$= £77\,250$$

Current value $\quad = £77\,250$

Representing the original value by 100%, the current value is represented by 103%.

*Multiplying by the scale factor 1.03 has the required **enlarging** effect on the original value.*

Repeated percentage changes

One advantage of the scale factor method is that the effect of repeated percentage changes is easily calculated.

Example

Over a period of three years, a property, originally priced at £120 000, increases in value by 4% in the first year, then increases by a further 7% in the second year, but suffers a 6% fall in value in the third year.

(a) What is its value at the end of the three years, correct to the nearest £1000?

(b) What is the overall percentage change in value?

(a) The required scale factors are 1.04, 1.07 and 0.94.

$$£120\,000 \times 1.04 \times 1.07 \times 0.94 = £125\,523.84$$

After three years, the property's value is £126 000 to the nearest £1000.

(b) Multiplying together the scale factors of the individual percentage changes gives the scale factor for the overall percentage change over the three-year period.

$$1.04 \times 1.07 \times 0.94 = 1.046\,032$$

This shows that the figure at the end of three years is 104.6032% of the original value, i.e. the overall percentage increase is 4.6% correct to 1 d.p.

Money that is invested will gain **compound interest** if all of the interest gained is added to the account to gain further interest. Compound interest involves repeated percentage change and the scale factor method greatly simplifies the calculations.

Example

£4000 is put into an account and gathers compound interest at 6.5% per year. What is the value of the account at the end of three years?

The scale factor for each year is 1.065

$$4000 \times 1.065 \times 1.065 \times 1.065 = 4000 \times (1.065)^3$$
$$= 4831.7985$$

Total in account at the end of three years is £4831.80 to the nearest penny.

Reverse percentages

The process of calculating the effect of a percentage change, by the scale factor method, may be represented on a diagram.

To undo the effect of this percentage change, and return to the original amount, this process must be reversed.

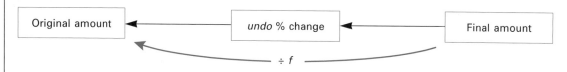

Example

The sale price of a jumper is £29.20. If the price has been reduced by 20% what was it before the reduction?

Using a diagram in the exam may help you to understand the problem and clarify the process.

Reversing the process is *not* the same as adding 20% onto the sale price.

Original price = £29.20 ÷ 0.8 = £36.50

Expressing one amount as a percentage of another

To convert any fraction or decimal into a percentage, multiply by 100%.
For example, $\frac{3}{5} = \frac{3}{5} \times 100\% = 60\%$ and $0.125 = 0.125 \times 100\% = 12.5\%$.

To express one amount as a percentage of another, first express as a fraction and then multiply by 100%. For example, to express 28.3 as a percentage of 41.2, calculate $\frac{28.3}{41.2} \times 100\%$. Using a calculator, this is keyed in as 28.3 ÷ 41.2 × 100, giving 68.7% correct to 3 s.f.

Calculator techniques

Order of operations

All scientific/graphic calculators operate under **algebraic logic**. Calculations are carried out using the rules of priority used in algebra whenever more than one operation is involved.

The order in which calculations are carried out is:

- brackets, i.e. calculations inside brackets are worked out first;

- powers and roots;

- multiplication and division;

- addition and subtraction.

You need to be aware of these priority rules so that you can plan a key sequence correctly. For example, $\dfrac{7.81 + 5.23}{8.67 - 2.39}$ means $(7.81 + 5.23) \div (8.67 - 2.39)$.

This may now be keyed in as it looks, followed by $\boxed{=}$ to give $2.076 \ldots = 2.08$ (correct to 3 s.f.). Alternatively, the first set of brackets may be omitted, provided that an extra $\boxed{=}$ is pressed before the $\boxed{\div}$.

An *estimate* may be obtained by replacing the given figures with figures of comparable size that are easier to work with. In the example above,

$$\frac{7.81 + 5.23}{8.62 - 2.39} \approx \frac{8 + 5}{9 - 2} = \frac{13}{7} \approx \frac{14}{7} = 2$$

In this case the estimate confirms the calculator result. If the expression had been keyed in *incorrectly* as $7.81 + 5.23 \div 8.62 - 2.39$ for example, giving $6.026 \ldots$, then it would be clear from the estimated value that an error had been made somewhere.

Special keys are used for squares, square roots and reciprocals, but other powers are found using the $\boxed{x^y}$ (or $\boxed{y^x}$) key and other roots may be found using the $\boxed{^x\sqrt{}}$ or $\boxed{x^{1/y}}$ key.

Examples

Expression	Possible key sequence	Value
2^7	2 $\boxed{x^y}$ 7 $\boxed{=}$	128
$\sqrt[4]{81}$	81 $\boxed{^x\sqrt{}}$ 4 $\boxed{=}$	3
$\sqrt{(47 \times 32)}$	$\boxed{\sqrt{}}$ $\boxed{(}$ 47 $\boxed{\times}$ 32 $\boxed{)}$ $\boxed{=}$	38.8 (3 s.f.)

An estimate is given by
$\sqrt{(49 \times 36)}$
$= \sqrt{49} \times \sqrt{36}$
$= 7 \times 6 = 42$.
The given figures have been replaced with larger ones so 42 is an over-estimate.

Accuracy

Measurements based on a **continuous** scale such as length, area, volume, weight or time can never be exact.

The degree of accuracy in a measurement is often stated to a given number of decimal places, or significant figures, in some units.

Example

Using an ordinary ruler with a metric scale it should be possible to measure a distance correct to the nearest 0.1 cm, i.e. to the nearest mm.

Suppose that the length of a pin is 2.3 cm to the nearest 0.1 cm. Using l cm to represent the length of the pin, the range of possible values in which l must lie is $2.25 \le l < 2.35$.

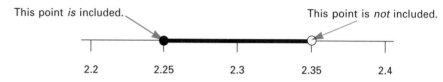

This point *is* included. This point is *not* included.

2.2   2.25   2.3   2.35   2.4

When **counting** is involved, as opposed to measurement, the situation is different. For example, if the number of pupils in a school is given as 950, to the nearest 10, then the upper bound value of 954 is included.

The values at the ends of the interval in which l must lie are known as the **bounds** of the interval. The **lower bound** is 2.25 and the **upper bound** is 2.35. The lower bound is included as a possible value for l but the upper bound is not.

In general, if a measurement is accurate to some given amount, then the maximum error is half of that amount. In the example above, the maximum error is half of 0.1 cm = 0.05 cm.

So the upper bound is given by 2.3 + 0.05 = 2.35 and the lower bound is given by 2.3 − 0.5 = 2.25.

Calculations involving error bounds

The upper and lower bounds of an expression, containing rounded values, can be worked out using the upper or lower bounds of these values as shown below. Using the notation X_{UB} and X_{LB} for the upper and lower bounds of X respectively:

- $(X + Y)_{UB} = X_{UB} + Y_{UB}$
- $(X + Y)_{LB} = X_{LB} + Y_{LB}$
- $(X - Y)_{UB} = X_{UB} - Y_{LB}$
- $(X - Y)_{LB} = X_{LB} - Y_{UB}$
- $(X \times Y)_{UB} = X_{UB} \times Y_{UB}$
- $(X \times Y)_{LB} = X_{LB} \times Y_{LB}$
- $(X \div Y)_{UB} = X_{UB} \div Y_{LB}$
- $(X \div Y)_{LB} = X_{LB} \div Y_{UB}$

It is better to try to understand how these rules work rather than to memorise them.

Example

If x = 1.2, y = 7.8 and z = 3.6 (all accurate to 1 d.p.) then:

- the upper bound of $\dfrac{x + y}{z} = \dfrac{1.25 + 7.85}{3.55} = \dfrac{9.1}{3.55} = 2.563\,38\ldots;$

- the lower bound of $\dfrac{x + y}{z} = \dfrac{1.15 + 7.75}{3.65} = \dfrac{8.9}{3.65} = 2.438\,356\ldots$

Questions

1 (a) List the prime numbers between 40 and 60.

   (b) Write 1400 as the product of its prime factors.

   (c) Given that $13\,230 = 2 \times 3^3 \times 5 \times 7^2$, find:

   (i) the HCF of 1400 and 13 230;

   (ii) the LCM of 1400 and 13 230.

2 Work out: (a) $\dfrac{8}{9} + \dfrac{5}{12}$ (b) $7\frac{1}{3} \div 5\frac{1}{2}$

3 Simplify $\dfrac{\frac{x}{3} - 1}{x - \frac{2}{3}}$.

4 (a) Write $37\frac{1}{2}\%$ as a fraction in its lowest terms.

   (b) Increase 560 by 7%.

5 What amount, when reduced by 23%, leaves 2849?

6 Given that $P = \dfrac{15.9 + 14.3}{\sqrt{98.7}}$:

   (a) Calculate the value of P correct to 3 s.f.

   (b) Estimate the value of P and compare it with the answer to part (a).

7 The length of the side of a square is measured as 12.8 cm, correct to 1 d.p.

   (a) State the upper and lower bounds for the length of the side.

   (b) Find the upper and lower bounds for the perimeter of the square.

   (c) Find the upper and lower bounds for the area of the square.

Solving numerical problems
Ratios

A **ratio** provides a means of comparing related quantities.

Example

Consider two lines L_1 and L_2. If the length of L_1 is 80 cm and the length of L_2 is 1.2 m, then the length of L_1 may be compared to the length of L_2 using a ratio.

The ratio of the length of L_1 to the length of L_2 is given by 80 cm to 1.2 m, which may be written as 80 cm : 1.2 m.

A ratio may be simplified by cancelling any common factors. If the quantities being compared are in the same units, then the units may also be cancelled.

Example

The ratio 80 cm : 1.2 m may be written as

80 cm : 120 cm = 2 : 3 in its simplest form.

Proportional division is the process of sharing an amount in a given ratio.

Example

The angles of a triangle are in the ratio 2 : 3 : 4. What are its angles?

$180° \div 9 = 20°$

$2 \times 20° = 40°$

$3 \times 20° = 60°$

$4 \times 20° = 80°$

> 2 + 3 + 4 = 9 and so we consider the angle sum to be made up of 9 parts. 180° ÷ 9 gives the value of each part.

The angles are 40°, 60° and 80°. (Check: 40° + 60° + 80° = 180°)

Information given as a ratio may be expressed in an **equivalent form** using fractions, decimals or percentages.

Example

Suppose that a sum of money is to be shared between A and B in the ratio 2 : 3.

(a) What is A's share as a fraction of B's share?

(b) What is A's share as a fraction of the whole amount?

(c) What is A's share as a percentage of the whole amount?

(a) $\frac{2}{3}$ (b) $\frac{2}{5}$ (c) $\frac{2}{5} \times 100\% = 40\%$

Proportion

Direct proportionality

If as two **variables** increase they remain in the same ratio to each other, then they are said to vary in **direct proportion**.

The statement 'y is directly proportional to x' is normally written as $y \propto x$ and may be interpreted as $\frac{y}{x} = k$, i.e. $y = kx$, for some constant k, known as the **constant of proportionality**.

Example

Pieces of electrical cable are cut from a large reel. The weight W (kg) of the pieces varies in direct proportion to their length L (m) as shown in the table below.

L	5	10	15	20	45
W	3.8	7.6	11.4	15.2	

In this case, $\frac{W}{L} = 0.76$, i.e. $W = 0.76L$.

When $L = 45$, $W = 0.76 \times 45 = 34.2$.

Alternatively, the columns in the table may be thought of as equivalent fractions, giving

$$\frac{15}{11.4} = \frac{45}{W},$$

i.e. $W = 11.4 \times 3 = 34.2.$

If $y \propto x$ and pairs of x and y values are plotted as coordinates, then the points will lie on a straight line through the origin. The gradient of the line gives the constant of proportionality.

In some situations, one variable may change in direct proportion to some **power** of the other. For example, taking the radius (r cm) of a circle as one variable, and the corresponding area (A cm^2) as the other, we have $A \propto r^2$ and the constant of proportionality is π.

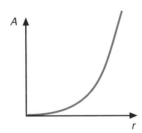

The graph of A against r is not a straight line. A is not proportional to r.

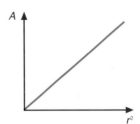

The graph of A against r^2 is a straight line. The gradient is $\frac{A}{r^2} = \pi$.

See the technique for converting an equation to linear form on page 32.

In general, if $y \propto x^n$, then plotting values of y on the vertical axis against values of x^n on the horizontal axis produces a straight line through the origin with gradient equal to the constant of proportionality.

Inverse proportionality

If as one variable increases the other *decreases* in such a way that their product remains constant, they are said to vary in **inverse proportion** to each other.

The statement 'y is inversely proportional to x' is represented by $xy = k$ for some constant of proportionality k. It follows that $y = \dfrac{k}{x}$ and we normally write $y \propto \dfrac{1}{x}$.

x	1	2	3	4	5	6
y	12	6	4	3	2.4	2

The table shows pairs of values of x and y values. In each case $xy = 12$.

Similarly, if y is inversely proportional to x^2, then

we write $y \propto \dfrac{1}{x^2}$ (i.e. $y \propto x^{-2}$).

In general, if $y \propto x^n$, then multiplying x by some number a has the effect of multiplying the corresponding value of y by a^n.

Examples

The volume of a sphere is directly proportional to the cube of its radius. If the radius is multiplied by 10 then the volume is multiplied by 1000, i.e. 10^3.

The electrical resistance of a wire is inversely proportional to the square of its diameter, $R \propto \dfrac{1}{d^2}$. Multiplying the diameter by 3 has the effect of multiplying the resistance by $\dfrac{1}{3^2} = 3^{-2}$, i.e. *dividing the resistance by 9.*

This links with the way in which areas and volumes of similar figures are related. See page 60.

Example

A frustrum of a cone is formed by removing a cone of height 4 cm from a cone of height 10 cm. The volume of the cone removed is 80 cm³. Find the volume of the frustrum.

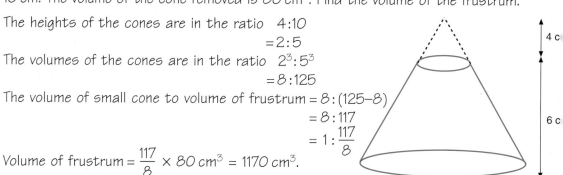

The heights of the cones are in the ratio $\quad 4{:}10$
$$= 2{:}5$$
The volumes of the cones are in the ratio $\quad 2^3{:}5^3$
$$= 8{:}125$$
The volume of small cone to volume of frustrum $= 8{:}(125{-}8)$
$$= 8{:}117$$
$$= 1{:}\dfrac{117}{8}$$

Volume of frustrum $= \dfrac{117}{8} \times 80 \text{ cm}^3 = 1170 \text{ cm}^3$.

4 c

6 c

Mixed problems

Standard form is often put into a context involving compound measures or percentages. In some cases, an exam question may specify that a calculator is not to be used and all working must be shown.

Example

Nuclear fusion at the centre of the Sun converts hydrogen to helium at the rate of 600 million tonnes per second, yet it is predicted to maintain its current brightness for another 6 billion years.

(a) Write 600 million in standard form.

(b) Calculate the mass of hydrogen used in 6 billion years.

(c) What percentage of the Sun's current mass, of 2×10^{27} tonnes, will have been converted to helium after 6 billion years?

(a) 600 million $= 600 \times 10^6$

$\qquad\qquad = 6 \times 10^2 \times 10^6$

$\qquad\qquad = 6 \times 10^8$ in standard form.

(b) Mass of hydrogen used is given by

$\qquad 6 \times 10^8 \times 60 \times 60 \times 24 \times 365 \times 6 \times 10^9$

$\qquad = 1.135\ 296 \times 10^{26}$

$\qquad = 1 \times 10^{26}$ tonnes (correct to 1 s.f.)

The information on which the calculation is based is only accurate to 1 s.f. and so it would not be sensible to give any greater accuracy in the answer.

(c) Percentage converted is given by

$\qquad \dfrac{1.135\ 296 \times 10^{26}}{2 \times 10^{27}} \times 100\% = 5.676\ldots\%$

$\qquad = 6\%$ correct to 1 s.f.

However, in subsequent calculations the unrounded value should be used to avoid introducing further error.

The final answer, again, is rounded to 1 s.f.

Example

The information given in the table may be used to compare some of the population characteristics of the United Kingdom with those of China and India.

Country	Area (km^2)	Population
China	9.57×10^6	1.18×10^9
India	3.29×10^6	9.03×10^8
UK	2.42×10^5	5.81×10^7

(a) Which of these countries has the greatest population?

(b) Which has the least?

(c) Which country has the greatest area?

(d) Round the given information to 1 s.f. and find the country with the lowest population density. *Do not use a calculator and show all your working.*

(a) China

(b) The United Kingdom

(c) China

The power of 10 determines the value of each number and should be considered first.

(d) Rounding to 1 s.f. gives:

China: $\dfrac{1 \times 10^9}{1 \times 10^7} = 1 \times 10^2$

$\qquad\qquad = 100$ people per km^2

The place values are the same for China and India but China's area is greater since 9.57 > 3.29.

India: $\dfrac{9 \times 10^8}{3 \times 10^6} = \dfrac{9}{3} \times \dfrac{10^8}{10^6} = 3 \times 10^2$

$\qquad\qquad = 300$ people per km^2

UK: $\dfrac{6 \times 10^7}{2 \times 10^5} = \dfrac{6}{2} \times \dfrac{10^7}{10^5} = 3 \times 10^2$

$\qquad\qquad = 300$ people per km^2

To compare the population densities of the UK and India requires the calculations to be worked to greater accuracy, but we have sufficient information to answer the question as given.

The country with the lowest population density is China.

The idea of a **percentage change** is one that may appear in a variety of guises on an examination paper. In general,

$$\text{percentage change} = \frac{\text{change in value}}{\text{original value}} \times 100\%$$

So,

$$\text{percentage profit} = \frac{\text{profit}}{\text{cost price}} \times 100\%$$

and

$$\text{percentage error} = \frac{\text{error}}{\text{true value}} \times 100\%.$$

When information is available to some given level of accuracy, the 'true value' may not be known but it is still possible to find the **maximum percentage error**.

Example

The length of a line is measured as 35 cm correct to the nearest cm. What is the maximum percentage error in the measurement?

The true value of the diameter lies in the interval shown.

34.5 35 35.5

The maximum percentage error is given by

$$\frac{0.5}{34.5} \times 100\% \quad = 1.449\ldots\%$$

$$= 1.45\% \text{ (correct to 3 s.f.)}$$

The maximum percentage error occurs when the true value lies at the lower end of the interval. This ensures the maximum value in the numerator and the minimum value in the denominator of the percentage error formula.

See page 20.

Solving numerical problems

Questions

1 Express these ratios in their simplest terms.

(a) 45 : 60   (b) 3 m : 20 cm
(c) 80 mm^2 : 50 cm^2 (d) $4\frac{1}{4} : 5\frac{2}{3}$

2 (a) Share £500 between A, B and C in the ratio 4 : 3 : 1.

(b) £90x is to be shared in the ratio $x - 5 : x : x + 5$. Given that the smallest share is worth £210, find the value of x.

3 Which of the following graphs shows that $p \propto q$? Give a reason for your answer.

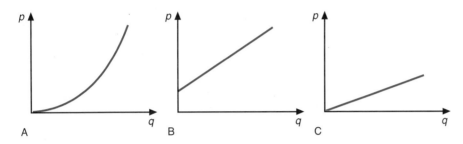

A   B   C

4 Given that $y \propto x^2$ and that y = 75 when x = 5, find y when x = 10.

5 Find the value of the following *without using a calculator*, and leave your answers in standard form.

(a) $(4 \times 10^{11}) \times (6 \times 10^7)$ (b) $(7.8 \times 10^{14}) + (4.6 \times 10^{15})$

6 The length (8.4 cm) and width (3.6 cm) of a rectangle are each known to be accurate to 1 d.p. Find the maximum percentage error in calculating the area of the rectangle.

Functional relationships
Using formulae

Examiner's tips and your notes

In the examination, you will be given a formula sheet like the one on pages 86–7. Make sure that you are familiar with all of the information given and the notation used.

When using a calculator, pay particular attention to the *order of operations* and remember that you may need to use brackets.

Avoid silly answers by using *estimation* as a rough check.

It is important that you have a calculator that you are used to for the examination.

Try the examples below and make a note of the key sequences needed on your calculator to obtain the given results.

Examples

Using $w = 5.6$, $x = -7.1$ and $y = 10.8$ find the value of these expressions:

(a) $\dfrac{w + x}{y}$ (b) $w - \dfrac{x}{y}$ (c) $\dfrac{w}{y - x}$

(d) $\sqrt{(w^2 + x^2)}$ (e) wx^2 (f) $(xy)^3$

Note that you may need to treat x^2 as $(-7.1)^2$ depending on your model of calculator.

Answers (correct to 3 s.f.):

(a) −0.139   (b) 6.26   (c) 0.313

(d) 9.04   (e) 282   (f) −451 000

Marks are awarded for showing your method.

If you use a formula to solve a problem, start by writing the formula and then substitute the values to make your method clear.

Example

Find the volume of this cone correct to one decimal place.

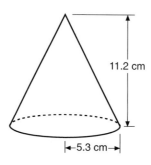

11.2 cm

←5.3 cm→

Volume of cone $= \frac{1}{3}\,\pi r^2 h$ From the formula sheet

$= \frac{1}{3}\,\pi \times 5.3^2 \times 11.2$ Substituting for *r* and *h*

$= 329.456 \ldots$

$= 329.5 \text{ cm}^3$ (to 1 d.p.)

Don't forget to round the answer to the required level of accuracy or you will lose marks.

Patterns and sequences

A **sequence** is a list of numbers in a particular order that follows some rule for producing further values. Each value in the list is referred to as a **term**.

The odd numbers form a sequence 1, 3, 5, 7, 9, 11, . . . in which the terms have a **common difference** of 2.

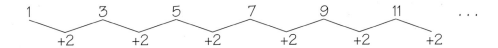

The **nth term** of a sequence is often denoted by u_n. For the odd numbers $u_n = 2n - 1$. So, for example, the 50th odd number is given by $2 \times 50 - 1 = 99$.

If the rule for the nth term of a sequence is **linear** (i.e. it takes the form $u_n = an + b$), then consecutive terms will have a common difference of a.

If the rule for the nth term is **quadratic**, then the first differences are not constant but the second differences are.

Example

An important example is the sequence of **triangle numbers**.

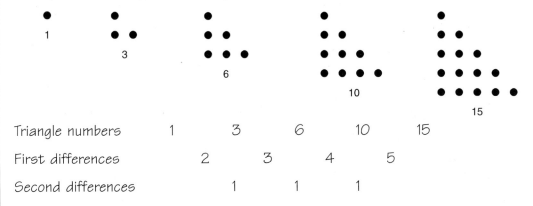

Triangle numbers	1		3		6		10		15
First differences		2		3		4		5	
Second differences			1		1		1		

Since the second differences for the triangle numbers are all the same, the rule for the nth term must be quadratic. In fact, the nth triangle number is given by $\frac{n}{2}(n + 1)$.

This is a useful result.

If the first and second differences are not constant, but the third differences are, then the rule for the nth term will be a **cubic**. This principle holds for higher powers.

A sequence such as 2, 4, 8, 16, 32, . . . is not of the same form as those above. The differences follow the same pattern as the original and the nth term is given by 2^n.

Graphs of equations

Graphs of linear equations

The most general form of a **linear** equation in x and y is ax + by = c. The graph of a linear equation is always a straight line and, conversely, the equation of any straight line can always be put into this form.

a, b and c may take any fixed values.

Examples

x = 3

y = −2

x + y = 5

In this case:

$a = 1, b = 0, c = 3$

In this case:

$a = 0, b = 1, c = -2$

In this case:

$a = 1, b = 1, c = 5$

You need to be familiar with this form of linear equation. Note that parallel lines have the same gradient.

Provided b ≠ 0, a linear equation may be written in the form **y = mx + c**. In this case the value of m gives the gradient of the line and the value of c gives the y-intercept.

Example

The equation 2x + 3y = 6 may be written as $y = -\frac{2}{3}x + 2$. It follows that the gradient is $-\frac{2}{3}$ and the y-intercept is at 2.

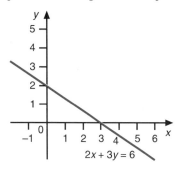

Note that the line slopes downwards from left to right showing that the gradient is negative.

A quick way to draw the graph of a linear equation is to find the coordinates of two points, for which the equation holds, and draw a straight line through them. For example, when x = 0, y = 2 and when y = 0, x = 3 so two points on the line are (0, 2) and (3, 0).

Graphs of quadratic equations

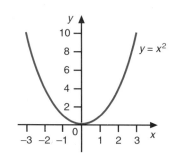

The graph of a non-linear equation will be a curve rather than a straight line. For example, the graph of $y = x^2$ is a special curve called a **parabola**.

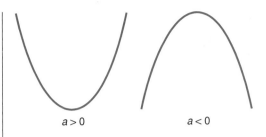

a > 0   a < 0

The general form of a **quadratic** expression is $ax^2 + bx + c$ where $a \neq 0$. Note that although a cannot equal zero, b and c can take *any* fixed values.

The graph of $y = ax^2 + bx + c$ ($a \neq 0$) is always a parabola which takes one of two possible forms depending on the value of a.

Example

Sketch the graph of $y = (x + 2)(x - 3)$.

To sketch the graph we need to recognise that this equation is simply a quadratic in factorised form (with $a > 0$). Since $y = 0$ when either $x = -2$ or $x = 3$ it follows that the curve must cross the x-axis at these values. In addition, the curve will cross the y-axis when $x = 0$, i.e. when $y = -6$.

> If you are asked to sketch a graph then you should show its basic shape and where it crosses the axes.

> Remember that a parabola has a **line of symmetry**.

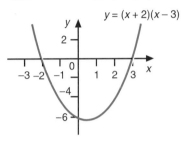

$y = (x + 2)(x - 3)$

Graphs of cubic equations

An equation of the form $y = ax^3 + bx^2 + cx + d$ where $a \neq 0$ is called a **cubic** equation. Once again, although a cannot equal zero, the other fixed values are unrestricted.

For $a > 0$ the graph of a cubic takes one of these forms:

> For a > 0 the overall trend is upwards from left to right.

For $a < 0$ the following forms are produced:

> This trend is reversed when a < 0.

Graph of $y = \dfrac{a}{x}$

The graph of $y = \dfrac{a}{x}$ takes two basic forms depending on the value of a.

For $a > 0$:   For $a < 0$:

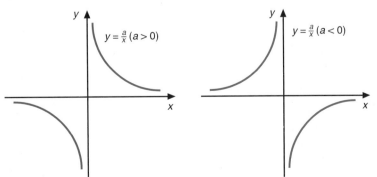

$y = \frac{a}{x} (a > 0)$ $y = \frac{a}{x} (a < 0)$

> Both $y = x$ and $y = -x$ are lines of symmetry. The curves also have rotational symmetry about $(0, 0)$.

Intersection of graphs

See page 40 for the algebraic approach to solving simultaneous equations.

If the graphs of two equations are drawn using the same axes, then any points at which the graphs intersect represent the simultaneous solution of those equations.

Examples

The second diagram also provides the solution of the quadratic equation $x^2 - 3x + 2 = 0$ since, at the points of intersection, $x^2 = 3x - 2$ (giving $x = 1$ or $x = 2$).

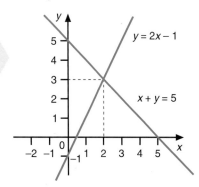

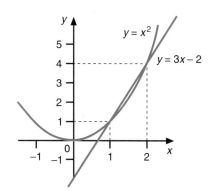

The simultaneous solution of $y = 2x - 1$ and $x + y = 5$ is $x = 2$ and $y = 3$.

Solving $y = x^2$ and $y = 3x - 2$ simultaneously we obtain two alternative pairs of x and y values: $x = 1$ and $y = 1$ or $x = 2$ and $y = 4$.

Finding relationships

This approach works particularly well when the values of x and y are inexact, such as when they are obtained by experiment.

If two variables x and y are related by a law of the form $y = ax + b$ then a graphical approach may be used to find the values of a and b using any known x and y values.

- Plot the x and y values as coordinates.

- Draw the *line of best fit*.

- Find the gradient of the line to obtain the value of a.

- Read off the y-intercept for the value of b.

Example

Use a graphical method to find an approximate linear relationship between the x and y values shown in the table.

x	10	20	30	40	50
y	19	24	30	40	46

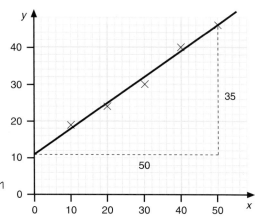

The points lie close to a straight line confirming that the relationship between x and y is approximately linear.

The gradient of the graph is $\dfrac{35}{50} = 0.7$ and the y-intercept is 11.

This suggests the relationship $y = 0.7x + 11$.

In the case where the law to be established is of the form $y = ax^2 + b$, the (x, y) coordinates, when plotted, will follow a curved path. However, it isn't easy to draw a curve of best fit and so the approach needs to be adapted.

The technique is to work out the values of x^2 and to plot these against the y values. In effect, this converts the equation to linear form ($y = aX + b$ where $X = x^2$) and so a line of best fit may then be drawn.

Once the line of best fit is established the values of a and b may be found as before.

Functions and transformations

Once the graph of a function is known, the graphs of related functions may be found by applying the appropriate transformations.

The transformations, given below, are applied to the graph of $y = f(x)$ in order to obtain the graph of the given function in each case.

You need to learn these results.

- $y = f(x) + a$ Translation given by $\begin{bmatrix} 0 \\ a \end{bmatrix}$

- $y = f(x + a)$ Translation given by $\begin{bmatrix} -a \\ 0 \end{bmatrix}$

- $y = kf(x)$ One-way stretch, with scale factor k, parallel to the y-axis.

    (If $k = -1$, this produces a reflection in the x-axis.)

- $y = f(kx)$ One-way stretch, with scale factor $\dfrac{1}{k}$, parallel to the x-axis.

    (If $k = -1$, this produces a reflection in the y-axis.)

Examples

The following graphs are based on the graph of $y = \sin x$.

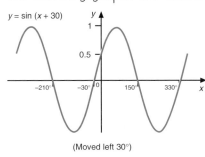
$y = \sin(x + 30)$

(Moved left 30°)

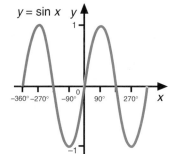
$y = \sin x$

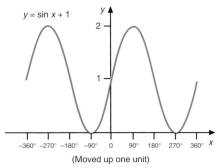
$y = \sin x + 1$

(Moved up one unit)

33

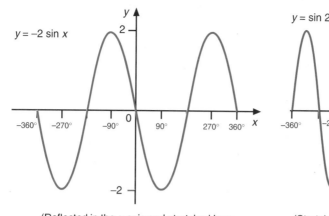

$y = -2 \sin x$

(Reflected in the x-axis and stretched by a factor of 2 parallel to the y-axis)

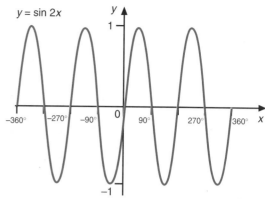

$y = \sin 2x$

(Stretched with factor $\frac{1}{2}$ parallel to the x-axis)

Interpreting area and gradient

Strictly speaking, velocity × time = **displacement**. However, the distinction is not significant when the velocity remains positive.

The **area** under a graph represents the product of the quantities on the two axes. For example, the area under a velocity–time graph (with velocity in m/s and time in s) represents velocity × time = distance (measured in m).

The area under a graph is calculated from measurements on the diagram, *using the appropriate scale for each axis.*

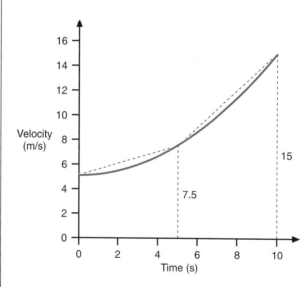

Example

The area under a curve may be found approximately by representing it as the sum of the areas of a number of trapeziums.

Using the two trapeziums shown gives the distance travelled in the first 10 seconds as
$\frac{5}{2}(5 + 7.5) + \frac{5}{2}(7.5 + 15) = 85$ m.

Greater accuracy may be obtained by using more trapeziums.

The **gradient** of a graph represents the rate of change of the quantity on the vertical axis with respect to the quantity on the horizontal axis. For example, the gradient of a velocity–time graph (with velocity in m/s and time in s) represents **acceleration** (measured in m/s²).

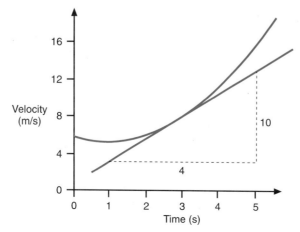

The gradient of a curve, at some point, is given by the gradient of the tangent to the curve at that point.

Example

Calculating the gradient of the tangent shown in the diagram gives the acceleration when $t = 3$ as 2.5 m/s².

Questions

1 The radius of a hemisphere is 21.6 cm.

    (a) Calculate its volume correct to 2 s.f.

    (b) Calculate the area of its curved surface correct to 3 s.f.

2 The first five terms of a sequence are 6, 13, 22, 33 and 46.

    (a) Find the first differences of these terms.

    (b) Use your answer to part (a) to find the second differences.

    (c) Find a formula for u_n, the nth term of the sequence. Simplify your answer.

3 A straight line has equation $3x + 2y = 8$.

    (a) Write the equation in the form $y = mx + c$.

    (b) State the gradient of the line.

4 Sketch the graph of the equation $y = (x + 2)(x - 1)(x - 3)$.

5 The values in the table below satisfy an approximate linear relationship of the form $y = ax + b$.

x	5	10	15	20
y	10.8	17.6	24.9	31.7

Use a graphical method to find the values of a and b.

6 The graph of the equation $y = x^2$ is translated 5 units to the right and 4 units up. State the equation of the graph produced.

Expressions involving **sums and differences** may be simplified by collecting **like terms**, i.e. terms in which the letters and powers are identical.

Examples

$$x + x = 2x \qquad x^2 + 2x^2 = 3x^2 \qquad 5x^2y - x^2y = 4x^2y$$

```
5(objects) - 1(object) = 4(objects)
  The 'objects' must be the same in
            each case.
```

$$5a - 7b^2 + 3a + b^2 + 4 = 8a - 6b^2 + 4 \text{ (This won't simplify further.)}$$

Note that an expression such as $3x + 4y - 2z + x^2 - xy$ cannot be simplified since there are no like terms.

Products of terms may also be simplified as shown in the examples below.

Examples

$$2 \times 3x = 6x \qquad\qquad 3x \times 4y = 12xy \qquad\qquad 3x \times 4x = 12x^2$$

$$2a^2 \times 3a^3 = 6a^5 \qquad\qquad 3ab^3 \times 2ab^4c = 6a^2b^7c \qquad -5x \times 3y = -15xy$$

```
Note that the
numbers are
multiplied ...
```

```
... but
powers of the
same letter
are added.
```

When **dividing**, powers of the same letter are subtracted.

Examples

$$x^5 \div x^2 = x^3 \qquad\qquad xy^2 \div x = y^2 \qquad\qquad xy \div y^3 = xy^{-2} = \frac{x}{y^2}$$

```
Each x is written without
  a power, meaning x¹.
Dividing gives x⁰ = 1,
which effectively means
  that the x's cancel.
```

```
In general y⁻ⁿ = 1 .
and so y⁻² = 1 . yⁿ
             y²
```

It is often easier to use fraction notation to simplify an expression involving division.

Example

Simplify $8x^2y \div 12x^3y$.

Rewriting as $\dfrac{8x^2y}{12x^3y}$ and **cancelling common factors** gives $\dfrac{2}{3x}$.

Expanding brackets

We often need to replace an expression containing brackets with an equivalent one in which the brackets have been removed – usually in order to simplify the expression.

Examples

$a + (b + c - d) = a + b + c - d$

If the sign outside the brackets is a '+' then the signs of terms inside the brackets are unchanged when the brackets are expanded.

$a - (b + c - d) = a - b - c + d$

However, a '−' sign outside the brackets has the effect of changing all the signs as the brackets are removed.

$a(b + c - d) = ab + ac - ad$

$-a(b + c - d) = -ab - ac + ad$

This principle also applies when multiplying out, so a positive term outside the brackets leaves the signs unchanged, whereas a negative term changes all the signs.

$(2x + 3)(x - 4)$
$= 2x^2 - 8x + 3x - 12$
$= 2x^2 - 5x - 12$

With double brackets, each term in the first is multiplied by each term in the second. The result can usually be simplified by collecting like terms.

> These are important results which should be learned.

$(a + b)^2 = a^2 + 2ab + b^2$
$(a - b)^2 = a^2 - 2ab + b^2$
$(a + b)(a - b) = a^2 - b^2$

A common error is to take $(a + b)^2$ to mean the same as $a^2 + b^2$.

Factorising

The *reverse* process of multiplying out brackets is known as **factorisation**. It is often used, for example, when rearranging formulae or solving equations.

$$\xrightarrow{\text{expand}}$$

$(a + b)(a - b)$ $a^2 - b^2$

$p(q + r)$ $pq + pr$

$$\xleftarrow{\text{factorise}}$$

To factorise an expression such as $pq + pr$, we need to 'take out' a **common factor** of both terms, in this case p.

To factorise a more complex expression *completely*, we first need to take out the **highest common factor**.

Example

Factorise $8pq^2r^3 - 12p^2q^2r$ completely.

$8pq^2r^3 - 12p^2q^2r$

$= 4pq^2r(2r^2 - 3p)$

The highest common factor is $4pq^2r$ which we take outside the brackets. We then complete the expression inside the brackets so that the result is equivalent to $8pq^2r^3 - 12p^2q^2r$.

Changing the subject

Changing the subject of a formula allows us to express it in the form best suited to a particular purpose.

The basic principle is that whatever action is taken on one side of the equation, in order to single out the new subject, the same action must be taken on the other side.

Example

Make l the subject of the formula $T = 2\pi\sqrt{\dfrac{l}{g}}$ and use the result to find l, correct to two significant figures, given that $T = 1$ and $g = 9.81$.

$T = 2\pi\sqrt{\dfrac{l}{g}}$ Divide both sides of the equation by 2π.

$\dfrac{T}{2\pi} = \sqrt{\dfrac{l}{g}}$ Square both sides, to remove the square root.

$\left(\dfrac{T}{2\pi}\right)^2 = \dfrac{l}{g}$ Multiply both sides by g.

$l = g\left(\dfrac{T}{2\pi}\right)^2$ Note that we normally write the subject on the left.

Substituting the given information into the new formula gives

$l = 9.81\left(\dfrac{1}{2\pi}\right)^2 = 0.248\,49\ldots = 0.25$ (to 2 s.f.).

> Remember to show your working and to round your answer to the required degree of accuracy.

When the new subject appears in more than one term, we gather those terms together on one side of the equation and take out the new subject as a common factor.

> Although r appears twice on the same side of the equation, it appears on different levels in the fraction.

Example

Make r the subject of the formula $p = \dfrac{r + a}{r + b}$.

$p = \dfrac{r + a}{r + b}$ The first move is to multiply both sides by $(r + b)$.

$p(r + b) = r + a$ Expand the brackets.

$pr + pb = r + a$ Collect the terms involving r on one side.

$pr - r = a - pb$ Factorise.

$r(p - 1) = a - pb$

$r = \dfrac{a - pb}{p - 1}$

> Note the combined use of expanding and factorising to solve the problem.

Simple equations and inequalities

Simple equations and inequalities may be solved by the rearrangement method used to change the subject of a formula.

< 'is less than'
> 'is greater than'
≤ 'is less than or equal to'
≥ 'is greater than or equal to'

Examples

Solve (a) $5x - 1 = 17 + x$ and (b) $5x - 1 < 17 + x$.

(a) $5x - 1 = 17 + x$	(b) $5x - 1 < 17 + x$	Take x from both sides.
$4x - 1 = 17$	$4x - 1 < 17$	Add 1 to both sides.
$4x = 18$	$4x < 18$	Divide both sides by 4.
$x = 4.5$	$x < 4.5$	

The solution of the inequality may be represented on a number line.

$x < 4.5$ 4.5

Use ● when the end point is included and ○ when the end point is not included.

When multiplying or dividing an inequality by a negative number, the direction of the inequality must be reversed; for example, if $-x \geq 5$ then $x \leq -5$.

Graphs of inequalities

The graph of an equation such as $y = 3$ is a line, whereas the graph of the inequality $y < 3$ is a **region** which has the line $y = 3$ at its **boundary**.

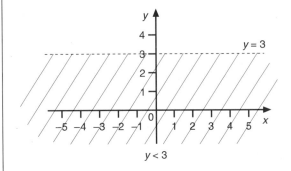

$y < 3$

To show the region for some given inequality, first draw the boundary line and then shade the points on one side. For *strict* inequalities < and > the boundary line is not included and should be shown as a dashed line.

Follow any instructions given on the exam paper and label your diagram clearly.

The solution of a problem may require us to locate a region that satisfies several inequalities simultaneously. In this situation it may be simpler to *shade out the unwanted regions* so that the solution is shown unshaded.

The diagram shows unshaded the region satisfying $y > 1$, $x \leq 4$ and $y \leq x$.

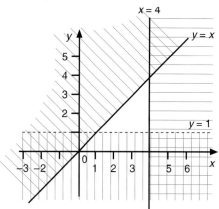

In **linear programming**, each point in the region identified represents a possible solution to a problem. We may then need to select the point that will maximise or minimise some expression.

For example, the maximum value of $x + y$ satisfying the given conditions is 8 (see the point $(4, 4)$).

Simultaneous equations

Solving a pair of equations simultaneously involves finding values for the letters that will make *both* equations work. This may be done algebraically or graphically.

See page 32 for the graphical approach.

The algebraic approach involves using the given information to produce a new equation containing only one of the unknown values. There are two main methods: by elimination or by substitution.

The elimination method

If the coefficient of one of the letters is the *same* in both equations, then that letter may be eliminated by *subtracting* the equations.

> In the expression $x - 5y$, the **coefficient** of x is 1 and the coefficient of y is -5.

Example

Solve simultaneously $2x + 3y = 6$ and $x + y = 1$.

$2x + 3y = 6$ ①	Labelling the equations makes it easier to show your method.
$x + y = 1$ ②	

② × 2 gives

$2x + 2y = 2$ ③	The coefficient of x is now the same in equations ① and ③.

① − ③ gives $y = 4$.

Substituting for y in ② gives $x + 4 = 1$, i.e. $x = -3$.	To find the value of x we now substitute the information that $y = 4$ in one of the original equations.

Solution is $x = -3$, $y = 4$.

Check your answer by substituting both values into the other equation:
$2x + 3y =$
$-6 + 12 = 6$.✓

If the matching coefficients have *opposite* signs, then the equations must be *added*.

Example

$5x - 3y = 26$ ①   The coefficients of y have equal size but opposite sign.

$2x + 3y = 2$ ②

① + ② gives $7x = 28$,

from which $x = 4$, $y = -2$.

The substitution method

In this method, information from one equation is substituted into the other.

Example

$3x - y = 9$ ①

$y = 2x - 4$ ②

Substituting for y in ① gives $3x - (2x - 4) = 9$ We need to remove the brackets and simplify.

$3x - 2x + 4 = 9$, i.e. $x + 4 = 9$ so $x = 5$.

Substituting for x in ② gives $y = 2 \times 5 - 4 = 6$.

The solution is $x = 5$, $y = 6$.   Checking in ① gives
$3 \times 5 - 6 = 9.$✓

Quadratic equations and inequalities

A quadratic equation is an equation of the form $ax^2 + bx + c = 0$ where $a \neq 0$.

If the graph of $y = ax^2 + bx + c$ is drawn then any points where the graph crosses the line $y = 0$ (i.e. the x-axis) represent solutions of the equation $ax^2 + bx + c = 0$.

See also 'Intersection of graphs' on page 32.

Examples

(a) $x^2 - x - 2 = 0$ (b) $x^2 + 6x + 9 = 0$ (c) $x^2 + 1 = 0$

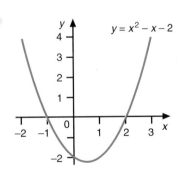

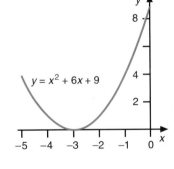

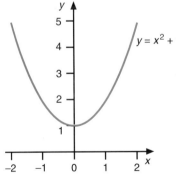

The solutions are $x = -1$ and $x = 2$.

The single solution is $x = -3$.

There are no solutions.

Diagram (a) also provides us with the solution of an inequality such as $x^2 - x - 2 \leq 0$. This corresponds to the values of x where the graph lies on or below the x-axis, i.e. $-1 \leq x \leq 2$.

Similarly, the values of x for which $x^2 - x - 2 > 0$ are seen to be $x < -1$ and $x > 2$.

Factorisation

Factorising a quadratic expression is often the first step when solving an equation, sketching a graph or solving an inequality in quadratic form.

Examples

(a) Solve $x^2 + 3x = 0$.   x is a common factor.

$x(x + 3) = 0$ In order for this product to be zero, either x is zero or $(x + 3)$ is zero.

$x = 0$ or $x = -3$

(b) Solve $x^2 - 5x + 4 = 0$.   Factorise using double brackets.

$(x - 1)(x - 4) = 0$ Either $x - 1 = 0$ or
          $x - 4 = 0$

$x = 1$ or $x = 4$

(c) Solve $14x^2 - 49x + 42 = 0$.   Divide throughout by 7.

$2x^2 - 7x + 6 = 0$ Factorise.

$(2x - 3)(x - 2) = 0$ Either $2x - 3 = 0$ or
          $x - 2 = 0$

$x = \dfrac{3}{2}$ or 2

(d) Solve $x^2 + x - 6 \geq 0$.   Factorise using double brackets.

$(x + 3)(x - 2) \geq 0$ Sketch the graph of $y = x^2 + x - 6$.

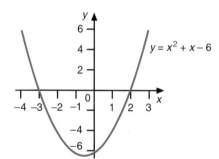

$y = x^2 + x - 6$

The sketch shows that the solution is in two parts.

$x \leq -3$ or $x \geq 2$

The quadratic formula

The formula is most useful when the quadratic expression cannot be factorised.

The solutions of $ax^2 + bx + c = 0$ where $a \neq 0$ are $x = \dfrac{-b \pm \sqrt{(b^2 - 4ac)}}{2a}$.

To solve $3x^2 - 5x + 1 = 0$ we need to recognise that $a = 3$, $b = -5$ and $c = 1$, giving

$x = \dfrac{5 \pm \sqrt{(25 - 12)}}{6}$

$x = \dfrac{5 + \sqrt{13}}{6}$ or $x = \dfrac{5 - \sqrt{13}}{6}$

$x = 1.434 \ldots$ or $x = 0.2324 \ldots$

$x = 1.43$ or $x = 0.232$ to 3 s.f.

Trial and improvement

The trial and improvement method for solving equations involves substituting selected values into one side of the equation to try to reach some target figure on the other. Solutions may be found to a high degree of accuracy using a systematic search.

Example

(a) Show that the equation $x^3 - 5x = 10$ has a solution between 2 and 3.

(b) Find this solution correct to two decimal places.

(a) When $x = 2$, $x^3 - 5x = 8 - 10 = -2$ which is too small.

When $x = 3$, $x^3 - 5x = 27 - 15 = 12$ which is too big.

It follows that $x^3 - 5x = 10$ for some value of x between 2 and 3.

(b)

x	$x^3 - 5x$	Comment
2.5	3.125	too small
2.8	7.952	too small
2.9	9.889	too small
2.95	10.922 375	too big
2.94	10.712 184	too big
2.91	10.092 171	too big

At this stage, the solution is trapped between 2.90 and 2.91. We now need to check the middle value. When $x = 2.905$, $x^3 - 5x = 9.990\ 36\ldots$ which is too small.

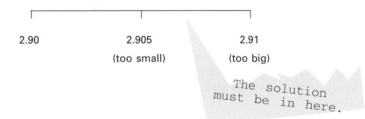

2.90	2.905	2.91
	(too small)	(too big)

The solution must be in here.

The diagram makes it clear that the solution is 2.91 correct to two decimal places.

Iteration

In the iterative method, the equation to be solved is first rearranged in the form $x = f(x)$ so that x is written as a function of itself. This result is then turned into an iterative formula $x_{n+1} = f(x_n)$.

The formula is used to produce a sequence that will converge to a solution of the original equation from a suitable starting value. Different rearrangements of the equation may be required to find further solutions.

Example

Consider the equation $3x^2 - 5x + 1 = 0$, previously solved using the formula.

We know that there are two solutions to this equation and so two rearrangements will be needed to find them.

First rearrangement:

$$3x^2 - 5x + 1 = 0$$

Add 5x to both sides
$$3x^2 + 1 = 5x$$

Divide both sides by 5
$$\frac{3x^2 + 1}{5} = x$$

Write as an iterative formula $\quad x_{n+1} = \dfrac{3x_n^2 + 1}{5}$

To use the formula you need a starting value i.e. a value for x_1. In the exam you will be told which value to use.

If you take $x_1 = 0$ then $x_2 = \dfrac{3 \times 0^2 + 1}{5} = 0.2$

$$x_3 = \frac{3 \times 0.2^2 + 1}{5} = 0.224$$

You can continue in this way to produce a sequence converging to the solution 0.23240812 to 8 decimal places.

This method works particularly well if your calculator has an ANS key. Key in 0 =   . (This sets ANS = 0 initially). Now key in (3 ANS^2 + 1) ÷ 5 and press the = key repeatedly to produce the sequence.

Note that not all starting values produce a convergent sequence. Try setting $x_1 = 2$. The numbers in the sequence rapidly get very large.

Second rearrangement:

The equation can be rearranged to give $x = \dfrac{5x - 1}{3x}$ so that $x_{n+1} = \dfrac{5x_n - 1}{3x_n}$.

You can check that this converges to 1.434258646 starting from $x_1 = 1$.

Questions

1 Simplify the following.

(a) $5x^2 - 3x + x^2 - 3x + 1$ (b) $\dfrac{25x^2yz^5}{15xy^3z^5}$.

2 (a) Remove the brackets and simplify $(x - 4)^2 - (3x + 2)$.

(b) Factorise $16x^2y^3 + 24xy^3z$ completely.

(c) Factorise $x^2 - y^2$.

(d) Factorise $16p^2 - 81q^2$.

3 Make T the subject of the formula $n = \dfrac{1}{2l}\sqrt{\dfrac{T}{m}}$.

4 Solve the inequality $\dfrac{5x}{3} - 2 < 4x + \dfrac{1}{3}$.

5 Solve the simultaneous equations $4x - 3y = 18$ and $3x + 2y = 5$.

6 (a) Factorise $x^2 + 2x - 35$.

(b) Solve $x^2 + 2x - 35 = 0$.

(c) Sketch the graph of $y = x^2 + 2x - 35$.

(d) Solve the inequality $x^2 + 2x - 35 < 0$.

7 (a) Use the quadratic formula to solve the equation $x^2 - 7x + 5 = 0$.

(b) Hence solve the inequality $x^2 + 5 < 7x$.

8 Show that the equation $x^3 - 2x = 19$ has a solution between 2 and 3. Find this solution, using a systematic search, correct to 2 d.p. and record the details of your progress in a table.

Congruent triangles

Examiner's tips and your notes

Two figures are said to be **congruent** if they are the same shape and size.

If a shape is cut out of a piece of card then congruent figures may be produced by drawing around the shape in different positions.

In solving a problem, we may need to recognise that two triangles are congruent and so it is useful to know a minimum set of conditions to look for.

A pair of triangles must be congruent if *any one* of the following sets of conditions is known to apply.

SSS The three sides of one triangle are the same in the other triangle.

SAS Two sides and the included angle in one triangle are equal to two sides and the included angle in the other.

AAS Two angles and a side in one triangle are equal to two angles and the corresponding side in the other.

RHS The triangles are right-angled and the hypotenuse and one side of one triangle are equal to the hypotenuse and one side in the other.

Examples

Not to scale

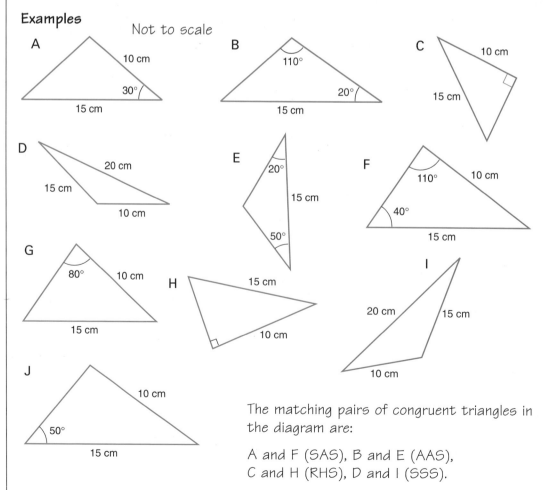

The matching pairs of congruent triangles in the diagram are:

A and F (SAS), B and E (AAS),
C and H (RHS), D and I (SSS).

Note that we do not have enough information to decide if G and J are congruent or not.

Angle properties of lines

Angles on one side of a straight line add up to 180°, i.e. a half turn.

Angles that meet at a point add up to 360°, i.e. a full turn.

When two straight lines cross, the vertically opposite angles formed are equal.

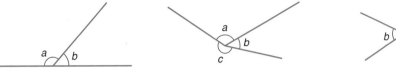

$a + b = 180°$ $a + b + c = 360°$ $a = d$ and $b = c$

When a line crosses some parallel lines, pairs of **corresponding angles** are equal and pairs of **alternate angles** are equal.

The pairs of corresponding angles shown are:

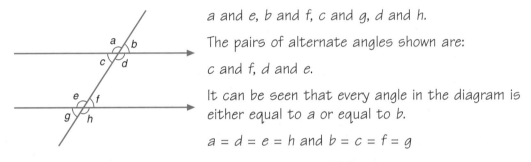

a and e, b and f, c and g, d and h.

The pairs of alternate angles shown are:

c and f, d and e.

It can be seen that every angle in the diagram is either equal to a or equal to b.

$a = d = e = h$ and $b = c = f = g$

Angle properties of polygons

A **convex** polygon is one in which all of the corners point outwards.

The sum of the **exterior angles** of any convex polygon is 360°.

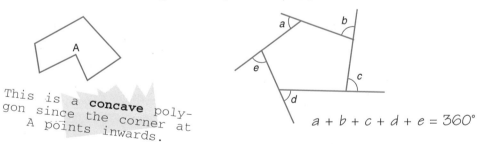

This is a **concave** polygon since the corner at A points inwards.

$a + b + c + d + e = 360°$

If a **regular polygon** with n sides has exterior angle θ then $n\theta = 360°$.

It follows that: $\theta = \dfrac{360°}{n}$ and $n = \dfrac{360°}{\theta}$.

At each vertex of a convex polygon, the **interior** and **exterior** angles add up to 180°.

The sum of the interior angles of any convex polygon with n sides is $(n - 2)\,180°$.

For example, the sum of the interior angles of a pentagon is $(5 - 2)\,180° = 3 \times 180° = 540°$.

For any triangle, the exterior angle is equal to the sum of the interior opposite angles.

$c = a + b$

Angle properties of the circle

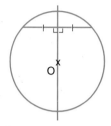

A line joining two points on the circumference of a circle is called a **chord**.

A chord divides a circle into two **segments**.

Some results follow from the symmetry of a diagram.

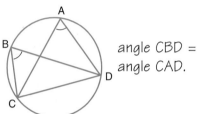

A line from the centre of a circle through the mid-point of a chord meets the chord at right angles.

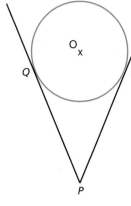

Tangents from the same point are equal. PQ = PR.

Angles in the same segment are equal.

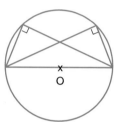

angle CBD = angle CAD.

A special case is that the angle in a semi-circle is always a right angle.

The **alternate segment theorem** states that the angle between a tangent and a chord drawn from the point of contact is equal to the angle in the alternate segment.

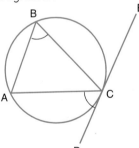

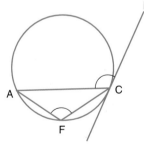

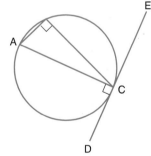

angle ACD = angle ABC.   angle ACE = angle AFC.   The tangent DE is at right angles to the diameter AC.

A quadrilateral which has all its vertices lying on the circumference of a circle is called a **cyclic quadrilateral**. Opposite angles of a cyclic quadrilateral add up to 180°.

The angle subtended at the centre of a circle by an arc is twice the angle subtended at the circumference by the same arc.

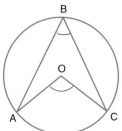

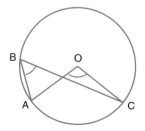

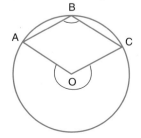

In each case, angle AOC = 2 × angle ABC.

Pythagoras' theorem

Pythagoras' theorem states that, in any right-angled triangle, the square on the hypotenuse is equal to the sum of the squares on the other two sides.

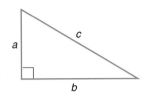

Many questions are based on the triples:

3, 4, 5

5, 12, 13

and 8, 15, 17.

Using the letters in the diagram, the theorem is written as $c^2 = a^2 + b^2$. This may be rearranged to give $a^2 = c^2 - b^2$ or $b^2 = c^2 - a^2$ which are useful for calculating the shorter sides.

Example

Find the length of the hypotenuse.

Using Pythagoras' theorem gives:

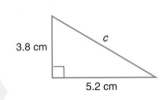

$$c^2 = 3.8^2 + 5.2^2$$
$$c^2 = 41.48$$
$$c = \sqrt{41.48}$$
$$c = 6.4404\ldots$$
$$c = 6.4 \text{ cm (to 2 s.f.)}$$

If the required degree of accuracy is not specified then be guided by the number of significant figures given in the question, when rounding your final answer.

Solving three-dimensional problems involves identifying, and working with, right-angled triangles in a particular plane.

Example

The diagram shows a square-based pyramid.

(a) Calculate the distance AP, where P is at the centre of the base.

(b) Given that V is directly above P, find the height of the vertex V above the base.

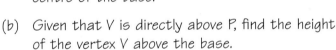

(a) Triangle ABC contains a right angle at B.

$$AC^2 = AB^2 + BC^2$$
$$= 10^2 + 10^2$$
$$= 200$$
$$AC = \sqrt{200}$$
$$AP = \tfrac{1}{2} \times \sqrt{200} = 7.071\ldots$$
$$AP = 7.1 \text{ cm (correct to 2 s.f.)}$$

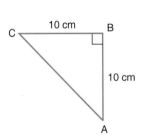

(b) Triangle VPA contains a right angle at P.

$$VP^2 = VA^2 - AP^2$$
$$= 144 - 50 = 94$$
$$VP = \sqrt{94} = 9.6953\ldots$$

Height of V above base = 9.7 cm (to 2 s.f.)

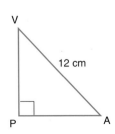

Trigonometry in right-angled triangles

The information given on the GCSE formulae sheet (see pages 87–8) applies to any right-angled triangle.

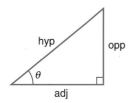

$$\sin \theta = \frac{\text{opp}}{\text{hyp}}$$

$$\cos \theta = \frac{\text{adj}}{\text{hyp}}$$

$$\tan \theta = \frac{\text{opp}}{\text{adj}}$$

Example

(a) Find the value of θ.

(b) Calculate the length BC.

(c) Calculate the length AC to 2 d.p.

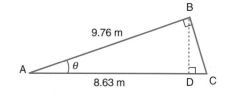

Angles should usually be rounded to 1 d.p. However, store the full value of θ in the calculator memory to minimise the error in parts (b) and (c).

(a) In triangle ABD, $\cos \theta = \dfrac{8.63}{9.76}$

giving $\theta = \cos^{-1}\left(\dfrac{8.63}{9.76}\right) = 27.844\ldots$

i.e. $\theta = 27.8°$ (to 1 d.p.)

(c) In triangle ABC, $\cos \theta = \dfrac{9.76}{AC}$

so $9.76 = AC \times \cos \theta$

i.e. $AC = \dfrac{9.76}{\cos \theta} = 11.037\ldots$

$AC = 11.04$ m (to 2 d.p.)

(b) In triangle ABC, $\tan \theta = \dfrac{BC}{9.76}$

$BC = 9.76 \times \tan \theta = 5.1554\ldots$

i.e. $BC = 5.16$ m (to 3 s.f.)

This result may be checked using Pythagoras' theorem.

As for Pythagoras' theorem, using trigonometry in three dimensions involves identifying, and working with, the appropriate right-angled triangles.

Example

Find the angle between the line AG and the plane ABCD in the diagram on the right.

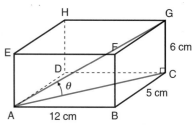

The sides of triangle ABC form the Pythagorean triple 5, 12, 13 and so AC = 13 cm.

This provides the necessary information in triangle ACG.

$\tan \theta = \dfrac{6}{13}$, i.e. $\theta = \tan^{-1}\left(\dfrac{6}{13}\right) = 24.77\ldots$

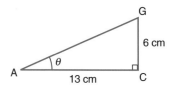

The required angle is 24.8° (to 1 d.p.)

Further trigonometry

The sine, cosine and tangent of 30°, 45° and 60° may be expressed exactly as shown below. These results are used extensively at A-level and familarity with them is recommended at this stage.

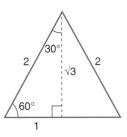 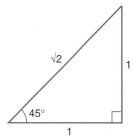

$$\sin 30° = \frac{1}{2} \qquad \sin 60° = \frac{\sqrt{3}}{2} \qquad \sin 45° = \frac{1}{\sqrt{2}}$$

$$\cos 30° = \frac{\sqrt{3}}{2} \qquad \cos 60° = \frac{1}{2} \qquad \cos 45° = \frac{1}{\sqrt{2}}$$

$$\tan 30° = \frac{1}{\sqrt{3}} \qquad \tan 60° = \sqrt{3} \qquad \tan 45° = 1$$

The definitions of sine, cosine and tangent, given for right-angled triangles, may be adapted so that angles outside the interval from 0° to 90° may be considered.

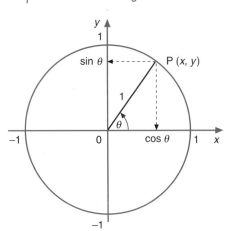

Consider a point P (x, y) on a circle with unit radius and centre O, such that OP makes an angle θ measured anti-clockwise from the positive direction of the x-axis.

For any angle θ, $x = \cos \theta$ and $y = \sin \theta$.

Using these results, $\tan \theta = \frac{y}{x} = \frac{\sin \theta}{\cos \theta}$.

These definitions are consistent with the earlier definitions used in right-angled triangles. For example, $\sin \theta = \frac{opp}{hyp} = \frac{y}{1} = y$.

Symmetry may be used to find angles that have the same sine, cosine or tangent.

A particularly important result is that, for any angle θ,

$$\sin \theta = \sin (180° - \theta)$$

This may be needed, for example, when using the **sine rule** to find an angle.

Examples

Find θ such that $\sin \theta = 0.8$ for $0° \le \theta \le 180°$.

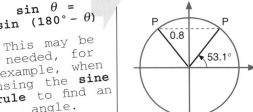

$\sin^{-1} (0.8) = 53.1°$ [from the calculator]

Using the symmetry of the diagram, another solution is $(180° - 53.1°) = 126.9°$

$\theta = 53.1°$ or $126.9°$ correct to 1 d.p.

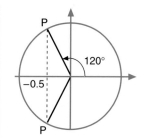

Solve cos θ = −0.5 for 0° ≤ θ ≤ 360°.

$\cos^{-1}(-0.5) = 120°$ [from the calculator].

Again, using symmetry, another solution
is (360° − 120°) = 240°

θ = 120° or 240°

Graphical representation

The behaviour of the sine, cosine and tangent functions may be represented
graphically as shown below.

y = sin x

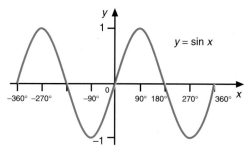

For any angle x, the value of sin x may
be found and lies between −1 and 1.

The graph has rotational symmetry of
order 2 about all of the points where it
crosses the x-axis.

y = cos x

> You need to be
> able to sketch
> the graphs of
> related
> functions such as
> y = 3 sin 2x.
> See pages 33–34.

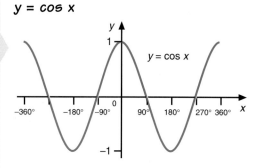

The cosine graph has the same shape,
and corresponding properties, as the
sine graph but is shifted 90° to the
left.

y = tan x

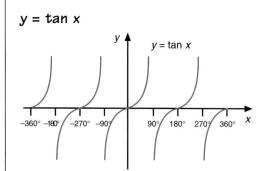

The value of tan x is given by $\dfrac{\sin x}{\cos x}$
and exists provided that
cos x ≠ 0.

The values of tan x repeat every 180°.

The graph has rotational symmetry of
order 2 about 0°, ±90°, ±180°, ±270°,
. . . on the x-axis.

The sine and cosine rules

Use of the sine and cosine rules allows us to solve problems in triangles that do not contain a right-angle. The rules are given on the formulae sheet (see pages 87–8).

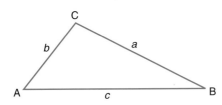

Sine rule
$$\frac{a}{\sin A} = \frac{b}{\sin B} = \frac{c}{\sin C}$$

Cosine rule $\quad a^2 = b^2 + c^2 - 2bc \cos A$

$$\cos A = \frac{b^2 + c^2 - a^2}{2bc}$$

It is important to recognise the convention used in labelling the triangle, i.e. the side labelled a is opposite angle A and so on. This needs to be remembered when using the rules to solve problems. In using the sine rule, for example, an equation is formed by setting:

$$\frac{\text{length of one side}}{\text{sine of opposite angle}} = \frac{\text{length of another side}}{\text{sine of its opposite angle}}$$

Using the sine and cosine rules

Example

Calculate the value of x in the diagram on the right.

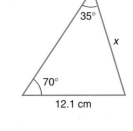

Using the sine rule gives

$$\frac{x}{\sin 70°} = \frac{12.1}{\sin 35°}$$

i.e. $x = \dfrac{12.1 \sin 70°}{\sin 35°} = 19.823\ 47 \ldots$

$x = 19.8$ cm (correct to 3 s.f.)

Example

Find the value of x and θ.

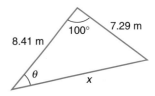

Using the cosine rule gives

$$x^2 = 8.41^2 + 7.29^2 - 2 \times 8.41 \times 7.29 \cos 100°$$

i.e. $x^2 = 145.164 \ldots$

so $x = 12.048 \ldots$

> Store the full value of x in the calculator memory for use later.

$x = 12.0$ m (correct to 3 s.f.)

> The form of the sine rule given on the formula sheet may be 'turned over' to find an unknown angle.

Using the sine rule now gives

$$\frac{\sin \theta}{7.29} = \frac{\sin 100°}{x}$$

i.e. $\sin \theta = \dfrac{7.29 \sin 100°}{x}$

> Use the stored value of x to avoid introducing unnecessary rounding errors.

$$\sin^{-1}\left(\frac{7.29 \sin 100°}{x}\right) = 36.5744 \ldots$$

so $\theta = 36.6°$ (correct to 1 d.p.)

> Note: 143.4°, i.e. (180° − 36.6°), is too large to be a possible solution in this case. See page 51.

Example

In some cases there may be two values of θ that satisfy the conditions given in a problem.

These diagrams are drawn to scale.

In each case $AB = 4.5\,cm$, $BC = 2.8\,cm$ and angle $CAB = 30°$.

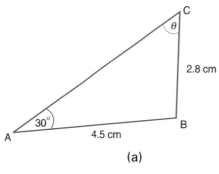

(a)

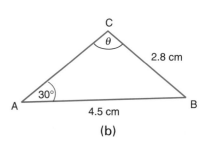

(b)

Using the sine rule in either triangle gives:

$$\frac{\sin \theta}{4.5} = \frac{\sin 30°}{2.8}$$

i.e. $\sin \theta = \dfrac{4.5 \sin 30°}{2.8}$

$\sin^{-1}\left(\dfrac{4.5 \sin 30°}{2.8}\right) = 53.47\ldots°$

In (a) θ is acute,   In (b) θ is obtuse,
so $\theta = 53.5°$ to 1 d.p.   so $\theta = 180° - 53.5°$
$= 126.5°$ to 1 d.p.

You can check these results by measuring the angles in the diagrams.

The area of a triangle

The area of any triangle is given by $\frac{1}{2}\,ab \sin C$, using the same convention for labelling the triangle as for the sine and cosine rules. Thus, the area of a triangle may be found whenever two sides and the included angle are known.

Example

See 'Area of a segment' on page 66.

Area $= \frac{1}{2} \times 5.8 \times 7.2 \sin 95° = 20.8005\ldots$

Area $= 21\ cm^2$ (correct to 2 s.f.)

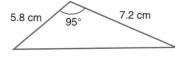

Not to scale

Questions

1 Given that the two triangles shown are congruent, find the values of x and **θ**.

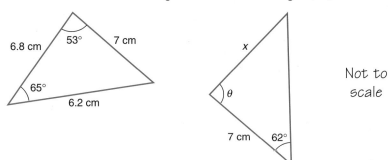

Not to scale

2 Each exterior angle of a regular polygon is equal to 18°. How many sides does it have?

3 Find the value of angles x and y.

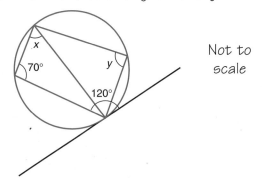

Not to scale

4 Find the values of x and y and the area of ΔBCD.

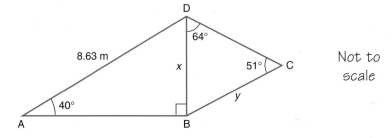

Not to scale

5 Find the exact values of **θ** between 0° and 360° such that

(a) $\sin θ = \dfrac{\sqrt{3}}{2}$ (b) $\cos θ = \dfrac{-1}{\sqrt{2}}$

6 Sketch the graph of y = 1 + sin 2x for values of x from 0° to 360°.

Vectors

A **vector** quantity is one that has **magnitude** (i.e. size) and **direction**. A quantity that has magnitude but no direction is a **scalar** quantity.

For example, numbers are scalars and the distance between two points is a scalar, but the **displacement** from one point to another is a vector.

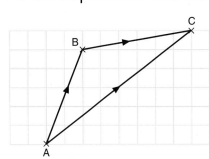

The vector from A to B is written as $\overrightarrow{AB}$.

In the diagram $\overrightarrow{AB} = \begin{bmatrix} 2 \\ 5 \end{bmatrix}$, $\overrightarrow{BC} = \begin{bmatrix} 6 \\ 1 \end{bmatrix}$ and $\overrightarrow{AC} = \begin{bmatrix} 8 \\ 6 \end{bmatrix}$.

Note that $\begin{bmatrix} 8 \\ 6 \end{bmatrix} = \begin{bmatrix} 2 \\ 5 \end{bmatrix} + \begin{bmatrix} 6 \\ 1 \end{bmatrix}$.

In general, $\overrightarrow{AC} = \overrightarrow{AB} + \overrightarrow{BC}$ and $\overrightarrow{AC}$ is described as the **resultant** of $\overrightarrow{AB}$ and $\overrightarrow{BC}$.

The magnitude of $\overrightarrow{AC}$ is given by $\sqrt{(8^2 + 6^2)} = 10$. In general, the magnitude of the vector $\begin{bmatrix} a \\ b \end{bmatrix}$ is given by $\sqrt{(a^2 + b^2)}$. This result is based on Pythagoras' theorem.

Points are always labelled with capital letters A, B, . . . but vectors may be labelled with lower-case letters **a, b,** . . . in **bold** print (these should be underlined <u>a</u>, <u>b</u>, . . . when written).

Vector algebra

For any choice of numbers, $a + b = b + a$ and $a + (b + c) = (a + b) + c$. The diagrams below illustrate the corresponding results for vectors.

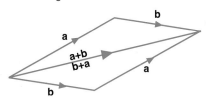

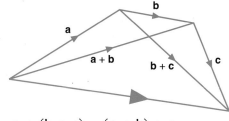

$a + b = b + a$

$a + (b + c) = (a + b) + c$

If **a** is any vector and k is a scalar, then k**a** is parallel to **a** but k times as long. If $k < 0$, then k**a** is in the opposite direction to **a**.

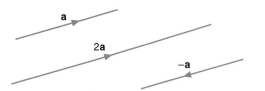

In column vector notation, if $\mathbf{a} = \begin{bmatrix} 4 \\ 2 \end{bmatrix}$ then $2\mathbf{a} = \begin{bmatrix} 8 \\ 4 \end{bmatrix}$ and $-\frac{1}{2}\mathbf{a} = \begin{bmatrix} -2 \\ -1 \end{bmatrix}$. The vectors $\begin{bmatrix} 4 \\ 2 \end{bmatrix}$, $\begin{bmatrix} 8 \\ 4 \end{bmatrix}$ and $\begin{bmatrix} -2 \\ -1 \end{bmatrix}$ are parallel.

The vector $\mathbf{a} - \mathbf{b}$ is the same as $\mathbf{a} + (-\mathbf{b})$ and this allows us to represent the subtraction of vectors on a diagram.

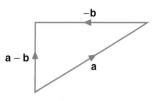

The **position vector** of a point P is the vector $\overrightarrow{OP}$ where O is the origin.

In the diagram the position vectors of A and B are $\mathbf{a}$ and $\mathbf{b}$ respectively.
Using this notation:

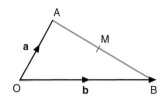

1) $\overrightarrow{AB} = \mathbf{b} - \mathbf{a}$

2) $\overrightarrow{OM} = \dfrac{\mathbf{a} + \mathbf{b}}{2}$ where M is the midpoint of AB.

You should learn these results.

Loci

The **locus** of a moving point is the set of positions it can occupy in order to satisfy some given conditions.

Example 1

The point moves so that it keeps a fixed distance d from point O.

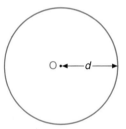

The locus is the set of points on the circumference of the circle with centre at O and radius d.

Example 2

The point moves so that its distance from a fixed point O is always less than d.

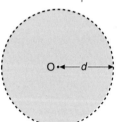

The locus is the **region** *inside* the circle. Points on the circumference define the boundary of the region, but are not included.

Example 3

The point moves so that it keeps a fixed distance d from a line AB.

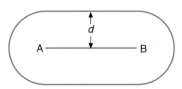

Semicircles with radius d are needed at the end points A and B.

Example 4

The point moves so that it is always a distance of at least d from each of the lines AB and BC.

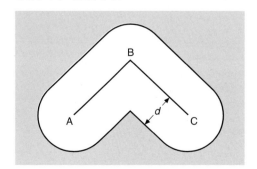

The locus is shown shaded and includes the points on the boundary.

57

Example 5

The point moves so that it is nearer to one of two fixed points than the other.

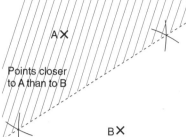

The dashed line shows the points equidistant from A and B and is known as the **mediator**. The locus of points closer to A than to B is shown shaded.

Example 6

The point moves so that it is equidistant from two intersecting lines.

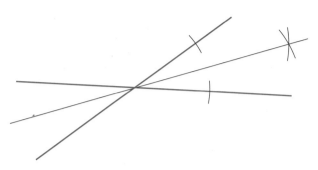

The locus is the line bisecting the angle between the given lines.

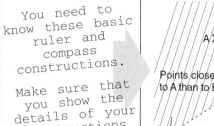

You need to know these basic ruler and compass constructions.

Make sure that you show the details of your constructions clearly.

Transformations

Knowledge of the four basic transformations **rotation**, **reflection**, **enlargement** and **translation** is required for the examination, together with simple combinations of these, such as two translations or a reflection followed by a rotation.

The shape to be transformed is often referred to as the **object** and may be labelled A, B, C, . . . The shape produced as a result of the transformation is referred to as the **image** and may be labelled A', B', C', . . . corresponding to the labelling of the object.

Rotation

To describe a rotation fully, the following details must be given:

- the *angle* through which the object is to be turned;

- the *direction* of movement: anti-clockwise (+) or clockwise (−);

- the *centre* of rotation, i.e. the point about which the movement takes place.

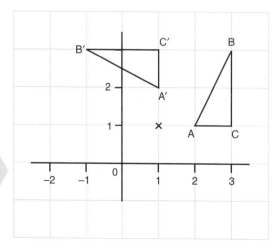

In the diagram, ΔABC is mapped onto ΔA'B'C' by a rotation of +90° about (1, 1).

Note that a rotation of −270° has the same effect as a rotation of +90°.

Every line of the object is rotated through the same angle to form the image.

Tracing paper may be used in the examination and can help you, for example, to locate the centre of rotation.

Reflection

A reflection is defined completely once the position of the mirror line is known. This is often done by giving the equation of the line, and the following forms are most commonly used: $x = a$, $y = a$, $y = x$ or $y = -x$.

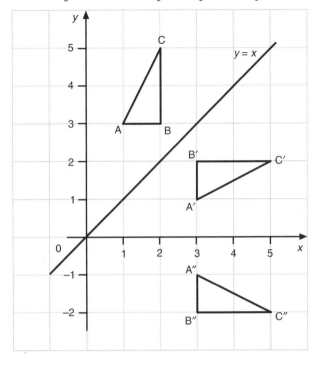

In the diagram, $\triangle ABC$ is mapped onto $\triangle A'B'C'$ by a reflection in the line $y = x$.

$\triangle A'B'C'$ is mapped onto $\triangle A''B''C''$ by a reflection in $y = 0$.

$\triangle ABC$ may be mapped onto $\triangle A''B''C''$ by a rotation of $-90°$ about $(0, 0)$.

The result given here, for $\triangle ABC$, applies to any figure; reflection in $y = x$ followed by reflection in $y = 0$ is equivalent to a rotation of $-90°$ about $(0, 0)$.

In general, a combination of two reflections is equivalent to a rotation about the intersection of the mirror lines.

Enlargement

To describe an enlargement, the scale factor and centre must be given. If the scale factor lies between 0 and 1 then the image will be smaller than the object, but the transformation is still classed as an enlargement.

Lines drawn through corresponding points on the object and image shapes meet at the **centre of enlargement**.

See also the section on similar figures on pages 60–61.

An enlargement preserves shape and so each angle in the object is equal to the corresponding angle in the image.

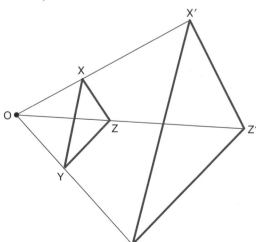

In the diagram, $\triangle XYZ$ is mapped onto $\triangle X'Y'Z'$ by an enlargement with centre at O and scale factor a for some $a > 1$.

If the **scale factor** of an enlargement is a, then each side of the image is a times as long as the corresponding side of the object; in the diagram, $X'Y' = a \times XY$.

The distance of any point on the image from O is a times as great as the corresponding point on the object from O; in the diagram, $OY' = a \times OY$.

$\triangle X'Y'Z'$ may be mapped onto $\triangle XYZ$ by an enlargement of scale factor $\frac{1}{a}$ with the same centre O.

If the scale factor of an enlargement is negative, then the image is drawn on the opposite side of the centre of enlargement to the object.

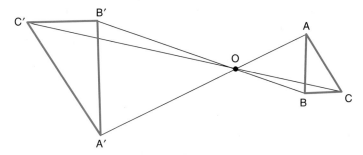

In the diagram, ΔABC is mapped onto ΔA'B'C' by an enlargement with scale factor −2 and centre at O.

ΔA'B'C' may be mapped onto ΔABC by an enlargement with scale factor $-\frac{1}{2}$ and centre at O.

Translation

A translation is a movement without any change of size or shape and without rotation. Vector notation may be used to describe a translation.

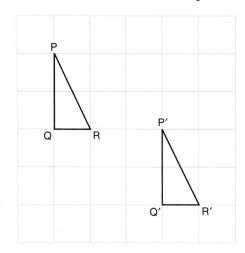

In the diagram, ΔPQR is mapped onto ΔP'Q'R' with a translation given by $\begin{bmatrix} 3 \\ -2 \end{bmatrix}$.

ΔP'Q'R' is mapped onto ΔPQR with a translation given by $\begin{bmatrix} -3 \\ 2 \end{bmatrix}$.

Similarity

Two figures are said to be **similar** if one may be regarded as an **enlargement** of the other. So figures with the same shape but different size are similar (whereas figures with the same shape and the same size are **congruent**).

For a given pair of similar figures, corresponding sides are in the same ratio. This ratio gives the **scale factor** for converting lengths of the sides of one figure into the corresponding lengths of the other.

Example

Find the value of x in the diagram, given that $\triangle ABC$ is similar to $\triangle ADE$.

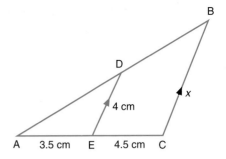

Equating the ratios of corresponding sides,

$$\frac{BC}{DE} = \frac{AC}{AE}, \text{ i.e. } \frac{x}{4} = \frac{8}{3.5}$$

giving $x = 4 \times \dfrac{8}{3.5} = 9.1428\ldots$

So x = 9.1 cm (correct to 2 s.f.)

> When comparing two quantities, a ratio of $a : b$ is often expressed as the corresponding fraction $\frac{a}{b}$.

> The value $\frac{8}{3.5} = 2.2857\ldots$ is the scale factor in this case.

Comparing areas and volumes

Areas of similar figures are *not* in the same ratio as corresponding lengths.

In the diagram, corresponding lengths are in the ratio 2 : 6 which simplifies to 1 : 3, whereas the areas are in the ratio 4 : 36 which simplifies to 1 : 9.

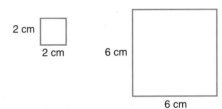

In this case, a length scale factor of 3 corresponds to an area scale factor of 9.

In general, if the corresponding lengths of two similar figures are in the ratio $a : b$, then their areas are in the ratio $a^2 : b^2$. This result may be expressed in the form

area scale factor = (length scale factor)^2

The principle may be extended to compare the *volumes* of similar objects which will be in the ratio $a^3 : b^3$. This result may be expressed in terms of scale factors as

volume scale factor = (length scale factor)^3

Example

If sphere A has volume 20 cm^3 and sphere B has twice its diameter, then the volume of sphere B is given by 20 cm$^3 \times 2^3 = 160$ cm^3.

> All spheres are similar. In this case, the volume scale factor is $2^3 = 8$.

Bearings

A **bearing** is an angle used to define direction of movement on the Earth's surface. The angle is measured from north in a clockwise direction and is given as a three-figure value.

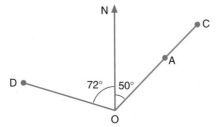

In the diagram, A and C both have a bearing of 050° from O.

The bearing of D from O is given by $360° - 72° = 288°$.

A **back bearing** gives the direction of movement needed for a return journey.

Example

A party of hill-walkers set off from A on a bearing of 235° to arrive at B. What bearing must they take to retrace their steps?

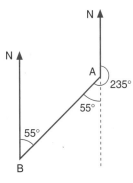

First represent the information on a sketch, including the north lines at A and B.

The north lines are parallel and so ∠NBA = 55° (alternate angles).

So to retrace their steps, the party must take a bearing of 055° from B.

Questions are often set on bearings that provide a context for the use of Pythagoras' theorem and trigonometry.

Example

A ship S sails from its harbour H to a point 16.8 km due east of a second ship T. Given that T is 10.4 km due south of H, find the bearing taken by S and the distance S travels.

Use a sketch to represent the information.

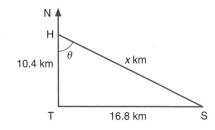

$$\theta = \tan^{-1}\left(\frac{16.8}{10.4}\right) = 58.24 \ldots$$

The required bearing is $180° - 58° = 122°$.

Using Pythagoras' theorem gives

$$x = \sqrt{(10.4^2 + 16.8^2)} = 19.758 \ldots$$

i.e. S travels 19.8 km (correct to 3 s.f.).

Example

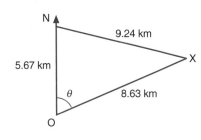

Find the bearing of X from O.

Using the cosine rule

$$\cos \theta = \frac{5.67^2 + 8.63^2 - 9.24^2}{2 \times 5.67 \times 8.63}$$

giving $\theta = 77.46 \ldots °$

So the bearing of X from O is 077°.

> The cosine rule may be used to find an angle when all three sides are known. There is only one angle in the range 0° to 180° with a given cosine.

Properties of position, movement and transformation

Questions

1   In the diagram AP = $\frac{1}{3}$ AB and BQ = $\frac{2}{3}$ BC.

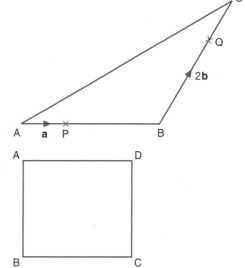

   (a) Express $\overrightarrow{AC}$ and $\overrightarrow{PQ}$ in terms of **a** and **b**.

   (b) Describe the relationship between the lines AC and PQ.

2   Using suitable constructions, show the locus of points, within the rectangle, that are at least as far from BC as AB, but nearer to D than A.

3   (a) Describe fully the transformations that will map:

     (i) ΔABC to ΔA′B′C′   (ii) ΔA′B′C′ to ΔA″B″C″

   (b) State the coordinates of the image of A under an enlargement with scale factor −3 and centre at (2, 0).

   (c) Show the image of ΔA″B″C″ under the translation $\begin{bmatrix} -6 \\ 1 \end{bmatrix}$ and label it A‴B‴C‴.

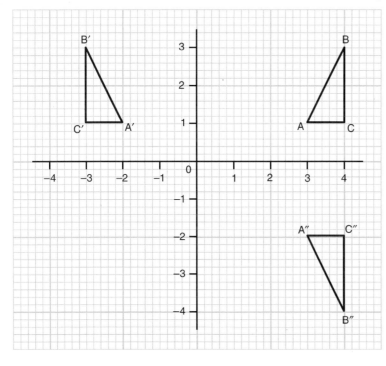

4   A small statue weighing 60 kg is to be reproduced on a larger scale. If the new statue is made out of the same material but three times as high, how much will it weigh?

5   A ship starts from a point Q, 53 km due south of a port at P, and sails on a bearing of 127° for 75 km to reach R.

   (a) How far is P from R?   (b) What is the bearing of P from R?

Measures

Conversions to know

Examiner's tips and your notes

Relationships *within* the metric and imperial systems must also be known. For example, 1 tonne = 1000 kg and 1 yard = 3 feet.

Questions may be set that require a knowledge of the relationship between metric and imperial units in common use. The following results should be *learned* as they are not given on the formulae sheet:

- 8 km ≈ 5 miles
- 1 m ≈ 39.37 inches
- 1 foot ≈ 30.5 cm
- 1 kg ≈ 2.2 lb
- 1 litre ≈ 1.75 pints
- 1 gallon ≈ 4.5 litres

Example

The length of a lawn is found to be 30 feet. What is its approximate length in metres?

30 feet = 30 × 12 in = 360 in

$$\frac{360}{39.37} = 9.14 \ldots$$

So the length of the lawn is approximately 9.1 m.

Compound measures

Distance and time are basic measures given in terms of single units such as metres and seconds respectively. Speed is an example of a **compound measure** since it is defined in terms of distance and time, requiring a mixture of the corresponding units.

Examples

$$\text{Average speed} = \frac{\text{distance}}{\text{time}}$$

If the distance is measured in metres, and time in seconds, then average speed

is measured in $\frac{\text{metres}}{\text{seconds}}$, i.e. metres per second (usually written as m/s or m s^{-1}).

$$\text{Density} = \frac{\text{mass}}{\text{volume}}$$

If mass is measured in kg and volume is measured in m^3 then density is measured in kg per m^3 (usually written as kg/m^3 or kg m^{-3}).

The **gradient** of a graph will be measured in terms of the units on the vertical and horizontal axes. For example, if a graph is drawn showing the volume of water in a swimming pool (in litres) on the vertical axis, against time (in hours) on the horizontal axis, then the gradient represents the **rate of change** of volume with respect to time in litres per hour.

Measurement of shapes

Formulae for the area and volume of the basic shapes are given on the formulae sheet (see pages 87–8). The information given below is not on the formulae sheet and should be *learned*.

Length of a circular arc

The length of a circular arc may be expressed as a fraction of the full circumference by considering the angle at the centre of the circle.

Example

Find the value of *l* correct to 1 d.p.

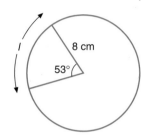

$$l = \frac{53}{360} \times \text{circumference}$$

$$= \frac{53}{360} \times \pi \times 16$$

$$= 7.400\ 19 \ldots$$

$$l = 7.4 \text{ cm correct to 1 d.p.}$$

Area of a sector

The shape enclosed between the arc of a circle and two radii is called a **sector**. The area of a sector is found by expressing it as a fraction of the area of the full circle.

Example

Express the area of the major sector as a multiple of π.

Area of major sector

$$= \frac{260}{360} \times \text{area of circle}$$

$$= \frac{260}{360} \times \pi \times 36$$

$$= 26\pi \text{ cm}^2$$

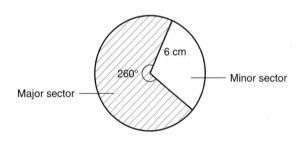

Area of a segment

The area of a segment is given by the difference between the area of the corresponding sector and the triangle formed by the chord and the radii.

Example

Find the area of the shaded segment correct to 3 s.f.

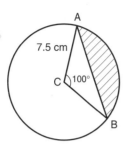

It is useful to remember that the area of any triangle is given by $\frac{1}{2} ab \sin C$. In the diagram, the area of $\triangle ABC$ is given by $\frac{1}{2} \times 7.5 \times 7.5 \sin 100°$

Area of shaded segment is given by

$$\frac{100}{360} \times \pi \times 7.5^2 - \frac{1}{2} \times 7.5^2 \sin 100°$$

$$= 21.389 \ldots$$

$$= 21.4 \text{ cm}^2 \text{ (correct to 3 s.f.)}$$

Volume of a prism

This is an important result. You need to recognise when to use it.

From the formulae sheet: Volume of prism = area of cross-section × length (see page 87).

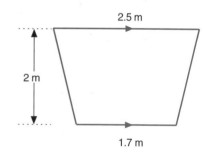

Example

The diagram shows the cross-section of a trench. The trench is 10 m long. Find its capacity.

Area of cross-section = $\frac{1}{2}(2.5 + 1.7) \times 2 = 4.2$ m^2

Capacity of trench = 42 m^3

Dimensions

- Distance is said to be **one-dimensional** since its measurement involves only units of **length**, i.e. (length)^1.

- Area is said to be **two-dimensional** since its measurement involves units of **length × length**, i.e. (length)^2.

- Volume is said to be **three-dimensional** since its measurement involves units of **length × length × length**, i.e. (length)^3.

- By contrast, number has **zero dimension**, i.e. it is **dimensionless**.

Dimensions and formulae

A consideration of dimensions allows us to distinguish between formulae for distance (e.g. perimeter), area and volume.

Example

A cone of height H and radius R has a cone of radius r removed to produce a **frustrum** of height h. Use the theory of dimensions to determine which of the following formulae must be *incorrect* (A represents the surface area of the frustrum and V represents its volume):

(a) $H = \dfrac{h + r}{R - r}$

(b) $H = \dfrac{hR}{R - r}$

(c) $A = \pi (R^2 - r^2) \sqrt{\dfrac{h^2}{(R - r)^2} + 1}$

(d) $A = \pi \sqrt{H^2 + R^2} - \pi \sqrt{(H - h)^2 + r^2}$

(e) $V = \dfrac{\pi h}{3} (R^2 + Rr + r^2)$

(f) $V = \pi (R^2 h + r)$

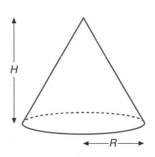

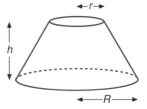

(a) The right-hand side (RHS) of the formula involves length ÷ length which is dimensionless, whereas the left-hand side (LHS) is one-dimensional.

(b) The RHS involves (length)^2 ÷ length, which is one-dimensional to match the LHS.

(c) The RHS involves number × (length)^2 × number, which is two-dimensional to match the LHS. Note that the expression under the square root includes (length)^2 ÷ (length)^2 which is dimensionless.

(d) The RHS involves the difference of terms of the form number × $\sqrt{(\text{length})^2}$, i.e. number × length, which is one-dimensional whereas the LHS is two-dimensional.

(e) The RHS involves number × length × (length)^2 which is three-dimensional and matches the LHS.

(f) The RHS includes (length)^3 + length which is meaningless.

It follows that (a), (d) and (f) must be incorrect.

It should be noted that even if the LHS and RHS of a formula have the same dimension this is no guarantee that the formula is correct.

Questions

1 The petrol tank of a car holds 15 gallons. Which of the following is closest to its capacity in litres? You must show your working.

50 l, 60 l, 70 l, 80 l

2 A rectangular block of wood measuring 30 cm × 8 cm × 6 cm weighs 1.5 kg. Calculate its density in kg/m^3.

3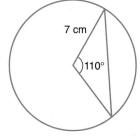

Calculate:

(a) the length of the arc of the major sector;

(b) the area of the minor sector;

(c) the area of the minor segment.

4 Of the four expressions given below, one represents a perimeter, one represents an area, one represents a volume and the other is meaningless. Use the theory of dimensions to distinguish between them. In each expression, x, y and z are all lengths.

$$\sqrt{x^2 + 2yz} \qquad \frac{x^2y - z^3}{x + y + xy} \qquad \frac{x^3 + x^2y + 5yz^2}{11\sqrt{2}} \qquad \frac{\pi(x^3 + y^3)}{x + 2y + 3z}$$

Handling data

Processing and interpreting data

Types of data

Examiner's tips and your notes

the distinction between discrete and continuous data is particularly significant when it is represented graphically. See pages 73-74.

Quantitative data is numerical in form and is taken to be **discrete** if only particular values may be included, or **continuous** if all values in some interval are possible. For example, the shoe sizes of a group of people are discrete, whereas the actual *lengths* of their feet are continuous (even when rounded) since they are measured on a continuous scale.

Qualitative data is descriptive, as opposed to numerical, in nature and is divided into **categories**. For example, the cars passing a checkpoint may be categorised by make or colour. Qualitative data may sometimes be referred to as **categorical data**.

Experiments, surveys and questionnaires

Experiments, surveys and questionnaires are different ways of gathering data for a particular purpose. The purpose may be made clear at the outset by stating a **hypothesis** to be tested.

Great care must be taken to avoid **bias** which will unfairly influence the data and may lead to false conclusions being drawn.

In an **experiment**, the possible **variables** must be recognised. The influence of a particular variable is isolated by making one change at a time and monitoring the results. All other conditions must remain constant throughout.

Example

An experiment might be devised to test the hypothesis that a new fuel additive improves the engine efficiency of a car. The amount of fuel used over a journey between two locations, for different concentrations of the additive, could provide the data but it would be necessary to eliminate the influence of a number of factors:

- the vehicle used,
- the route followed,
- the style of driving (speed/acceleration, etc.),
- the traffic conditions,
- the weather conditions.

The first three are examples of controlled variables and the last two are uncontrolled variables.

In a **survey**, or **questionnaire**, data is collected without any attempt to control or manipulate any outcomes.

In addition to the usual considerations for courtesy, the questions used in a questionnaire should:

You may be asked to criticise some examples of questions used in a questionnaire or to provide some of your own.

- be clear and unambiguous;
- produce data in a form that may be analaysed;
- avoid any suggestion of a 'right' answer;
- allow for a full range of responses whenever options are presented.

Sampling

The complete group of persons, objects or items related to some statistical enquiry is known as a **population**.

An efficient way of finding information about a population is to select a **sample** for analysis. Care must be taken to avoid **bias** in the selection of the sample so that it is **representative** of the population.

A sample needs to be large enough to provide reliable information about the population, but small enough to be manageable. A rough guide is to select a sample consisting of between 5% and 10% of the population.

There are several methods of selecting a sample and, in some situations, one may be more appropriate than another.

Two of the most commonly used methods are described below.

Random sampling

To produce a **random sample**, every member of the population must have an *equal* chance of being selected.

One way to select members of a population at random is to assign a number to each member and then use one of the standard techniques for generating random numbers in the required range.

Scientific calculators will produce random numbers between 0 and 1, usually to 3 d.p. The numbers shown below were produced in this way.

Graphical calculators may be programmed to produce random numbers automatically in any specified range.

0.348
0.115
0.22
0.557
0.745
0.685

This should be regarded as 0.220 so that the zero isn't missed out.

Suppose that we wish to produce random numbers in the range 0 to 70. This could be done, for example, by selecting the digits after the decimal point in pairs and ignoring any that are too big. In this way, the given numbers would produce:

34, 81, 15, 22, 05, 57, 74, 56, 85

giving 34, 15, 22, 5, 57 and 56.

Stratified sampling

When a population is comprised of a number of separate groups (known as **strata**) it may be desirable that each group is represented *proportionately* within the sample. A sample produced in this way is said to be **stratified**.

Example

Suppose that a company employing 120 women and 31 men is to undergo some changes on which the views of the workforce are sought.

A basic random sample of 10% would consist of 15 people but may not have a fair balance of men and women. However, a stratified 10% sample would be made up of 12 women selected at random and 3 men selected at random.

> Selecting a stratified sample eliminates one possible source of bias.

Representing data

> Conventions regarding the construction of statistical diagrams do vary. The details given below represent the most common practice.

Patterns, trends and relationships within data are often made clearer through the visual impact of appropriate diagrams and graphs.

Conversely, inappropriate use of diagrams and graphs can distort the information and present a misleading picture.

Example

The two diagrams represent the same information but, in the second, the changes are exaggerated because the vertical scale doesn't start at zero.

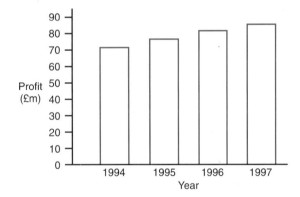

> If the scale on either axis doesn't start at zero then attention should be drawn to this fact using a jagged line, like this:

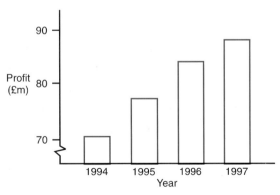

Pie charts

In a pie chart, each sector represents a category as a *proportion* of the whole. For example, if in a survey, 73 people are questioned and 11 give a response in a certain category, then the angle of the corresponding sector is calculated as

$$\frac{11}{73} \times 360° = 54.24 \ldots° = 54° \text{ (to the nearest degree)}.$$

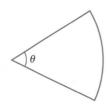

If the angle of a sector is θ, then the sector represents $\frac{\theta}{360}$ of the whole.

For example, if the angle of a sector representing the amount of a typical day that a person watches television is 30° then the actual amount of time that this corresponds to is given by $\frac{30}{360} \times 24$ hours = 2 hours.

Line graphs

There are different kinds of line graph that may serve different purposes. The diagram below shows how joining isolated data points with straight lines can make it easier to see trends.

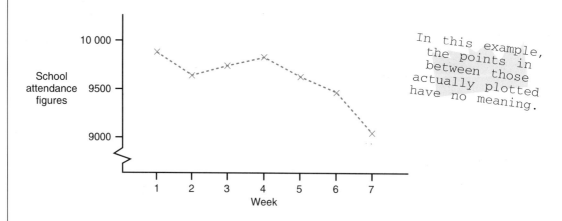

In this example, the points in between those actually plotted have no meaning.

Frequency diagrams

Bar graphs

Bar graphs may be used for both qualitative data and discrete data. In a frequency diagram, the vertical axis represents frequency and the bars have gaps between them.

In the case of discrete data, the bars are sometimes replaced with vertical lines to produce a **bar-line graph**.

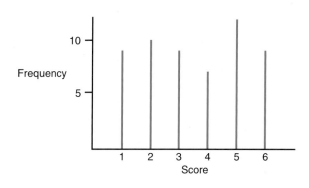

Frequency polygons

The table below shows a **frequency distribution** of test scores.

Score	0–9	10–19	20–29	30–39	40–49	50–59
Frequency	3	8	12	20	16	4

The data has been **grouped** into **class intervals** and may be represented using a **frequency polygon**.

The frequency polygon is formed by plotting the mid-point of each interval against the corresponding frequency and joining the points with straight lines. The mid-points may be found by adding the end-points and dividing by 2. So, for example, the mid-point of the 10–19 interval, is given by (10 + 19) ÷ 2 = 14.5.

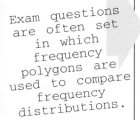

Exam questions are often set in which frequency polygons are used to compare frequency distributions.

Since the data is discrete in this case, the end-points of the class intervals are as given in the table.

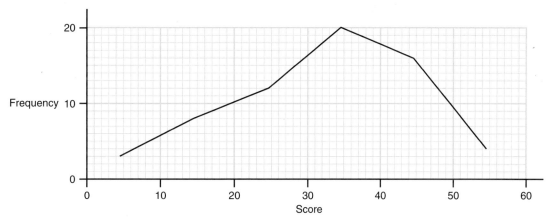

Cumulative frequency diagrams

A cumulative frequency diagram may be used to represent both discrete and continuous data. In either case, the data must be **grouped** into **classes** and the **upper boundary** of each class is plotted against the cumulative frequency.

Watch for any special instructions given on the exam paper.

A **cumulative frequency polygon** is produced by joining the plotted points with straight lines. Alternatively, a smooth curve may be drawn through the points to produce a **cumulative frequency curve** known as an **ogive**.

Example

Fifty pupils who walk to school were asked to time their journey to the nearest minute. The grouped data is shown in the table below.

Time (min)	Frequency	Cumulative frequency
0–10	3	3
11–20	15	18
21–30	18	36
31–40	10	46
41–50	3	49
51–60	1	50

Cumulative frequency diagrams may be used to find information about the data. See pages 79–80.

Remember to use the upper boundaries.

Since the data is *continuous* in this case, the upper boundaries are 10.5, 20.5, . . . and the corresponding points to plot are (10.5, 3), (20.5, 18), . . .

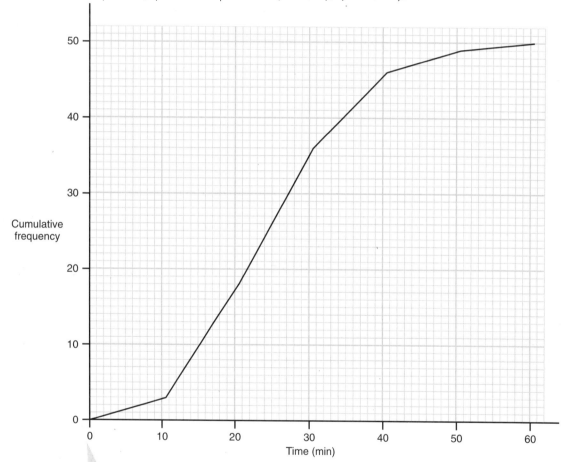

The graph starts at (0, 0) since there are no pupils who arrive in less than zero minutes.

Histograms

A **histogram** is used to represent the distribution of continuous data that has been grouped into classes. It resembles a bar chart in appearance but it is the area of a bar that represents frequency and there are no gaps between the bars.

Typically, data is distributed thinly at the extremes and so the outlying classes may be made wider, resulting in *bars of unequal width*. The height of each bar is then determined by its **frequency density** where:

$$\text{frequency density} = \frac{\text{frequency}}{\text{class width}}$$

> In the *special case* where the bars are all of equal width, the height of the bars may be used to represent frequency.

Example

The data used for the cumulative frequency diagram may be represented using a histogram. In the table below, two of the original classes have been combined.

Time (min)	Frequency	Frequency density
0–10	3	3 ÷ 10.5 = 0.29
11–20	15	15 ÷ 10 = 1.5
21–30	18	18 ÷ 10 = 1.8
31–40	10	10 ÷ 10 = 1
41–60	4	4 ÷ 20 = 0.2

> The class width is the difference between the boundary values of the class; e.g. 60.5 − 40.5 = 20.

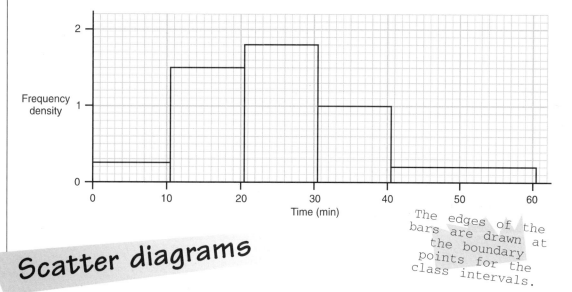

> The edges of the bars are drawn at the boundary points for the class intervals.

Scatter diagrams

A **scatter diagram** may be drawn to illustrate the relationship between two variables. Data is collected in pairs, one value for each variable, and plotted as coordinates. The distribution of the plotted points gives an indication of any relationship that exists and is described in terms of the **correlation** between the variables. The closer the plotted points lie to a straight line, the stronger the correlation.

Positive correlation   Negative correlation   Zero correlation

As one variable increases, so does the other.   As one variable increases, the other decreases.   There is no relationship between the variables.

A **line of best fit** may be drawn to represent the relationship. The line should be central to the distribution and have roughly the same number of points above it as below it. When the correlation between a pair of variables is strong, the line of best fit may be used to estimate the value of one variable for some given value of the other.

Example

An archaeologist discovers a bone, 25.3 cm long, from the forearm of a 1000-year-old skeleton of a man and wants to estimate how tall he would have been.

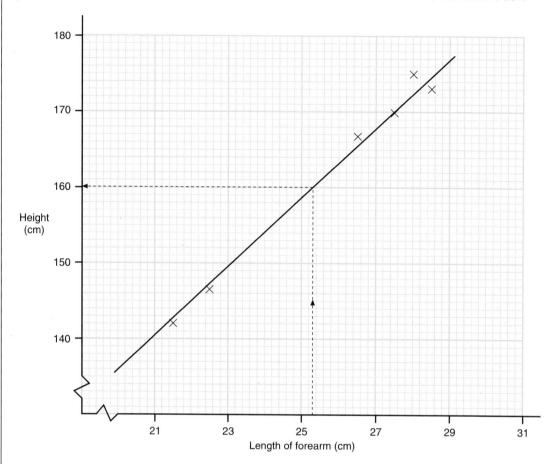

In this scatter diagram, each cross represents a person.

The diagram shows a strong positive correlation between length of forearm and height.

Using the line of best fit, the man is estimated to have been about 160 cm tall.

Analysing data

Averages

You need to know how the averages are defined and to appreciate the need for more than one form.

An **average** is a value that is taken to be typical, i.e. representative, of a set of data. It is sometimes described as a **measure of central tendency**.

There are several ways of working with data in order to produce an average. The three forms of average needed for the GCSE exam are the **mean, median** and **mode**. In some situations one form of average may be more appropriate than another.

The mean

The mean is found by adding all of the values together and dividing the result by the number of them.

One advantage of the mean is that it takes account of every individual element of data. A disadvantage is that it may be heavily influenced by extreme values.

The median

The median is the value in the middle of the data when it is *arranged in order of size*. If there are n elements of data, then the *position* of the median (i.e. not its value) is given by $\frac{n + 1}{2}$. In the case where n is even this should be interpreted as the value half-way between the middle pair.

The median has the advantage that it isn't affected by extreme values but, as a disadvantage, it can be quite insensitive to changes in the data.

The mode

The mode (or modal value) is simply the value that occurs with the greatest frequency.

The mode requires no calculation and is particularly easy to find if the data is presented in a frequency table. It works best when one value, out of a limited number of possibilities, appears significantly more often than any other. However, it is possible, for example, that several values may occur with the same highest frequency in which case the mode is inappropriate.

Example

The number of children in a sample of 50 households is shown in the table below.

Number (n)	Frequency (f)	$n \times f$
0	6	0
1	14	14
2	19	38
3	8	24
4	3	12
Totals	50	88

mean = $\frac{88}{50}$ = 1.76

median = 2 (25th, 26th values both = 2)

mode = 2 (occurs most often)

Dispersion

Dispersion is a term that refers to the **spread** of the data. Two samples of data may have very similar averages, but one may be quite widely spread and the other have all its values clustered around the average.

The range

The simplest measure of dispersion is the **range**, which is the difference between the smallest and largest values. The problem with the range is that it is dependent on the extreme values only, and may not be representative of the general spread.

The interquartile range

The **interquartile range** is a measure of spread across the 'middle half' of the data and so avoids the problem, described above, with using the range.

The **quartiles** Q_1, Q_2 and Q_3 divide the data into four equal parts (Q_2 is the median).

The **lower quartile** Q_1 is in the middle of the lower half of the data and, similarly, the **upper quartile** Q_3 is in the middle of the upper half of the data.

Interquartile range = upper quartile – lower quartile

Example

Data: 21, 23, 27, 27, 29, 30, 31, 32, 32, 32, 52

Range = 52 – 21 = 31

Interquartile range = 32 – 27 = 5

> The interquartile range gives a better representation of the spread of the data than the range.

The standard deviation

> In the exam, you may be asked to compare two samples of data. In this case, you will be expected to use an average and a measure of dispersion.

The **standard deviation** measures the spread of data around the mean and has the advantage that every element of data is taken into account. This is a very important statistical measure used in advanced work.

Formulae for the standard deviation use **sigma notation** to simplify what is written. The Greek capital letter Σ (sigma) stands for the **sum** of terms of a particular form.

The formulae sheet provided in the examination gives the standard deviation s as:

$$s = \sqrt{\frac{\Sigma(x - \bar{x})^2}{n}} \quad \text{or} \quad s = \sqrt{\frac{\Sigma x^2}{n} - \left(\frac{\Sigma x}{n}\right)^2}$$

> Scientific calculators have a statistical mode which allows the data to be entered. The values of $\bar{x}$ (the mean), Σx^2 (the sum of the squares) and the standard deviation can then be obtained directly. The symbol used for standard deviation varies from one calculator to another.

These formulae are equivalent, but the second one tends to be easier to work with. The expression inside the square root may be thought of as the *mean of the squares minus the square of the mean*.

Make sure that you know how to obtain these results on your machine.

Example

For the data 5, 6, 8, 8, 9, 9, 9, 9, 10, 11

$\overline{x} = 8.4$ $\Sigma x^2 = 734$ $s = \sqrt{\dfrac{734}{10} - 8.4^2}$

$s = 1.685$ (correct to 4 s.f.)

When comparing sets of data, larger values of s mean that the data is more widely dispersed.

Suppose that every value in a set of data is transformed so that $x \rightarrow ax + b$ to produce a new set of data.

The new values of the mean and standard deviation can be worked out from the old values:

* New $\overline{x} = a \times (\text{old } \overline{x}) + b$ * New $s = a \times (\text{old } s)$

Notice that adding a fixed number to every data value doesn't change the standard deviation.

Example

Using the results above we can find the mean and standard deviation of these sets of data.

(a) 15, 16, 18, 18, 19, 19, 19, 19, 20, 21
     $\overline{x} = 8.4 + 10 = 18.4$, $s = 1.685$

(b) 10, 12, 16, 16, 18, 18, 18, 18, 20, 22
     $\overline{x} = 2 \times 8.4 = 16.8$, $s = 2 \times 1.685 = 3.37$

Analysing grouped data

When data is grouped, we do not have exact information to work with and so we can only identify the modal class and find estimates for the mean, standard deviation, median and interquartile range.

Estimating the mean and standard deviation

The technique is to use the mid-point of each class interval to represent the class.

Example

The heights of a group of year 11 pupils are shown in the table.

Height (h cm)	Frequency (f)	Mid-point (x)	fx	fx^2
$140 \le h < 150$	1	145	145	21025
$150 \le h < 160$	5	155	775	120125
$160 \le h < 170$	7	165	1155	190575
$170 \le h < 180$	12	175	2100	367500
$180 \le h < 190$	6	185	1110	205350
Total	31	Total	5285	904575

The modal class is $170 \le h < 180$. This class also contains the median.

In a frequency table $n = \Sigma f$, Σx becomes Σfx and Σx^2 becomes Σfx^2

An estimate of the mean is $\dfrac{5285}{31} = 170.483 \ldots = 170$ cm (correct to 3 s.f.)

An estimate of the standard deviation is $\sqrt{\dfrac{904575}{31} - \left(\dfrac{5285}{31}\right)^2}$

$= 10.7279 \ldots$

$= 10.7$ cm to 3 s.f.

You can find the mean and standard deviation from your calculator but make sure that you show enough working to justify your answers.

Estimating the median and interquartile range

Estimates of the median and interquartile range can be obtained from a cumulative frequency graph.

Example

Using the data of the previous example:

Height (h cm)	Frequency	Cumulative frequency
$140 \leq h < 150$	1	1
$150 \leq h < 160$	5	6
$160 \leq h < 170$	7	13
$170 \leq h < 180$	12	25
$180 \leq h < 190$	6	31

For n elements of data, the lower quartile, median and upper quartile correspond to the $\frac{1}{4}(n + 1)$th, $\frac{1}{2}(n + 1)$th and $\frac{3}{4}(n + 1)$th positions respectively.

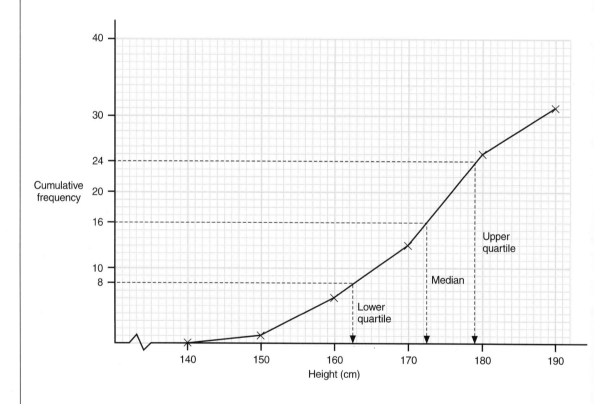

Lower quartile = 162.5 cm

Median = 172.5 cm

Upper quartile = 179 cm

Interquartile range = 16.5 cm

When n is large, $(n + 1)$ is replaced with n. So, for example, if $n = 1000$ then the median is taken to be in the 500th position. Correspondingly, the lower and upper quartiles would be in the 250th and 750th positions.

Questions

1 Describe a situation in which it would be more appropriate to use stratified sampling than random sampling.

2 A school operates a system in which merits are awarded for good work. The number of merits awarded to year 7 pupils during the first and last half-terms of the school year are shown in the table.

Number of merits	Half-terms	
	first	last
0–10	4	19
11–20	16	27
21–30	34	68
31–40	87	39
41–50	38	26
51–60	9	9

(a) Draw two frequency polygons on the same axes to represent the data.

(b) Estimate the mean number of merits awarded in each half-term.

(c) Compare the distribution of merits in the two half-terms.

3 Explain why the interquartile range is a more reliable measure of dispersion than the range.

4 (a) Calculate the mean and standard deviation of the data given below.

   11, 14, 12, 18, 16, 12, 17, 16, 16, 13, 11, 18, 17, 10, 14

(b) Describe the effect, on the mean and standard deviation, of adding a fixed number n to each value in the data.

(c) Write down the mean and standard deviation of:

   11.8, 14.8, 12.8, 18.8, 16.8, 12.8, 17.8, 16.8, 16.8, 13.8, 11.8, 18.8, 17.8, 10.8, 14.8

Probability

In any situation involving chance, there are a number of possibilities or **outcomes** that may actually occur. Some outcome, or combination of outcomes, may be of particular interest and is described as an **event**.

The **probability** of an event is a measure of the *likelihood* that the event will occur, expressed as a number from 0 to 1.

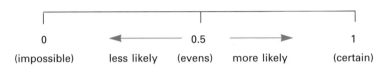

0		0.5		1
(impossible)	less likely	(evens)	more likely	(certain)

An outcome is said to be **favourable** to an event if it satisfies the conditions defining the event. For example, when an ordinary six-sided dice is thrown, the possible outcomes are 1, 2, 3, 4, 5 and 6. If we let A represent the event of obtaining an odd score then the outcomes favourable to A are 1, 3, and 5.

A **fair** dice or coin, for example, is one that is **unbiased** and will produce results at **random**; all of the outcomes are **equally likely** but the order in which they will occur cannot be predicted.

In a situation where each of the possible outcomes is equally likely, the probability that an event A occurs, written as P(A), is given by:

$$P(A) = \frac{\text{number of outcomes favourable to A}}{\text{total number of possible outcomes}}$$

For example, the probability that an odd score is obtained using an unbiased dice is expressed as:

$$P(\text{odd score}) = \frac{3}{6} = \frac{1}{2}$$

Mutually exclusive events are events that cannot happen together. Such events have no favourable outcomes in common. If A and B are mutually exclusive events, then the probability that one of them will happen is given by:

$$P(A \text{ or } B) = P(A) + P(B)$$

If events A_1, A_2, A_3, . . ., A_n are mutually exclusive and, between them, they account for all possible outcomes, then $P(A_1) + P(A_2) + P(A_3) + . . . + P(A_n) = 1$.

For any event A, the event '**not A**' describes the event that A will not occur. These events are clearly mutually exclusive and, since one of them must happen:

$$P(A) + P(\text{not A}) = 1, \text{ i.e. } P(\text{not A}) = 1 - P(A).$$

Independent events are events that can happen together but have no influence on each other. If A and B are independent events, then the probability that they happen together is given by:

$$P(A \text{ and } B) = P(A) \times P(B)$$

> This result may be extended to any number of independent events.

Example

A biased dice for which the probability of scoring 6 is given by P(6) = 0.4 is thrown with a fair coin. What is the probability of obtaining 6 together with heads?

The outcome for the dice has no influence on the outcome for the coin, and vice versa, so the events are independent.

$$P(6 \text{ and heads}) = P(6) \times P(\text{heads}) = 0.4 \times \tfrac{1}{2} = 0.2$$

Tree diagrams

Tree diagrams are a useful way of representing combined events.

Example

A bag contains 3 red marbles and 7 blue marbles. A marble is selected at random, and replaced, then a second marble is randomly selected.

(a) What is the probability that both marbles are red?

(b) What is the probability that the marbles are different in colour?

In this case, probabilities for the second selection are unaffected by the outcome of the first; the diagram shows independent events.

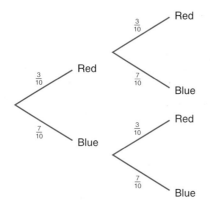

> Each route through the diagram corresponds to a particular combination of events. Probabilities are multiplied along the branches to give the combined probability of the events on the route.

> Two routes satisfy the given condition and so the corresponding probabilities must be added.

(a) $P(\text{both red}) = \tfrac{3}{10} \times \tfrac{3}{10} = \tfrac{9}{100}$

(b) $P(\text{different colours}) = \tfrac{3}{10} \times \tfrac{7}{10} + \tfrac{7}{10} \times \tfrac{3}{10} = \tfrac{42}{100} = 0.42$

Tree diagrams may also be used when the probabilities at the second stage are **conditional** on the outcomes of the first, i.e. when the events are **dependent**.

Example

The diagram below shows how the previous example is changed when the first marble selected is *not replaced*.

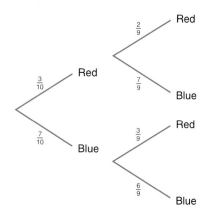

Once the probabilities are assigned to the branches, the tree diagram is used as before.

$$P(\text{both red}) = \frac{3}{10} \times \frac{2}{9} = \frac{1}{15} \qquad P(\text{different colours}) = \frac{3}{10} \times \frac{7}{9} + \frac{7}{10} \times \frac{3}{9} = \frac{7}{15}$$

In general, if A and B are two events such that B depends on A then:

$$P(A \text{ and } B) = P(A) \times P(B \text{ after } A \text{ has happened}).$$

Two-way tables

In the exam, information may be presented in the form of a two-way table.

Example

The table shows the results of a survey of students in a sixth form.

	Male	Female	Totals
Wears glasses	8	12	20
Does not wear glasses	32	37	69
Totals	40	49	

Find the probability that a student selected at random:

(a) is male, (b) wears glasses, (c) is male and wears glasses.

(a) $\frac{40}{89}$ (b) $\frac{20}{89}$ (c) $\frac{8}{89}$

Result (c) may be obtained directly from the table but note that $\frac{40}{89} \times \frac{20}{89} \neq \frac{8}{89}$, showing that the events are not independent.

Alternatively:

P(male and wears glasses) = P(male) × P(wears glasses given that the person is male)

$$= \frac{40}{89} \times \frac{8}{40} = \frac{8}{89}$$

Relative frequency

For a fair coin P(heads) = 0.5. However, if the coin is tossed 10 times then 'heads' may be obtained on 7 occasions giving a **relative frequency** of

$\frac{7}{10}$ = 0.7.

In an experiment, the relative frequency of an event only becomes a reliable indicator of its probability for a *large* number of **trials**.

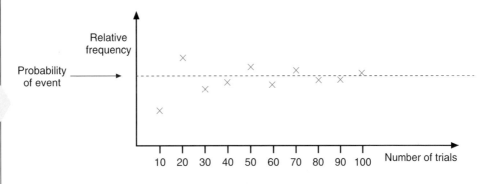

e diagram shows
ow the relative
requency values
'settle' towards
the probability
of the event
when the number
of trials is
increased

Regarding each trial that produces an outcome favourable to the event as a success we have:

$$P(event) \approx \frac{\text{number of successes}}{\text{total number of trials}}$$

This result may be used to predict the number of successes for a given number of trials:

$$\text{Expected number of successes} = P(event) \times \text{number of trials}$$

Again, this is only a reliable result when the number of trials is large.

Estimating probability

Whenever the possible outcomes of a situation are not equally likely, the standard definition of probability breaks down.

Weather forecasts will often include a prediction about the likelihood of rain, expressed as a probability. This cannot be worked out using equally likely outcomes and is, in fact, an estimate based on comparison with historical records for similar conditions.

In any situation where a process is repeated many times, the probability of a particular event may be estimated using a variation of the result given earlier:

$$P(event) = \frac{\text{number of successes}}{\text{total number of observations}}$$

Estimating and calculating the probabilities of events

Questions

1 A, B and C are three events such that $P(A) = \frac{3}{4}$, $P(B) = \frac{2}{3}$ and $P(C) = \frac{1}{5}$.

(a) Given that A and C are mutually exclusive events, find P(A or C).

(b) Explain why A and B cannot be mutually exclusive events.

(c) Given that $P(A \text{ and } B) = \frac{1}{2}$, show that events A and B are independent.

2 (a) Complete the tree diagram to find the probability that, if two fair dice are thrown, *exactly* one will show a score of six.

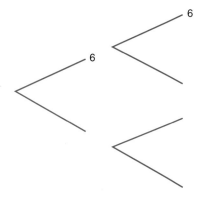

(b) Find the probability of scoring no sixes when *three* dice are thrown.

(c) What is the probability of obtaining at least one six with three dice?

3 Two of the most popular A-level courses in a particular school's sixth form are maths and history.

	Maths	Not maths
History	7	18
Not history	21	56

What is the probability that a student, selected at random, studies:

(a) maths and history,

(b) maths but not history,

(c) history given that the student doesn't study maths?

4 One of the activities at a school fund-raising event involves rolling three dice, with a prize for scoring less than 5 in total.

(a) What is the probability of winning?

(b) What is the expected profit if 500 people each pay 50p and a prize is worth £10?

Formula sheet

Area of triangle $= \frac{1}{2} \times base \times height$

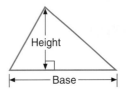

Area of parallelogram $= base \times height$

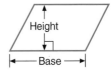

Area of trapezium $= \frac{1}{2}(a + b)h$

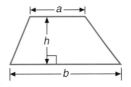

Volume of cuboid $= length \times width \times height$

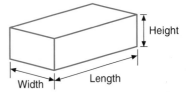

Volume of prism $= area\ of\ cross\text{-}section \times length$

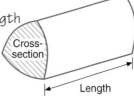

Volume of cylinder $= \pi r^2 h$

Area of curved surface of cylinder $= 2\pi rh$

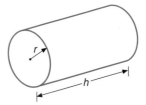

Volume of sphere $= \frac{4}{3}\pi r^3$

Surface area of sphere $= 4\pi r^2$

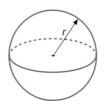

Volume of cone $= \frac{1}{3}\pi r^2 h$

Curved surface area of cone $= \pi rl$

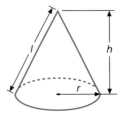

Pythagoras' theorem

$$a^2 + b^2 = c^2$$

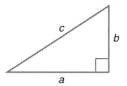

Circumference of circle $= \pi \times$ diameter

$$= 2 \times \pi \times \text{radius}$$

Area of circle $= \pi \times (\text{radius})^2$

Trigonometry

$$\sin\theta = \frac{\text{opp}}{\text{hyp}}$$

$$\cos\theta = \frac{\text{adj}}{\text{hyp}}$$

$$\tan\theta = \frac{\text{opp}}{\text{adj}}$$

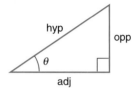

In any triangle ABC

Sine rule $\quad \dfrac{a}{\sin A} = \dfrac{b}{\sin B} = \dfrac{c}{\sin C}$

Cosine rule $a^2 = b^2 + c^2 - 2bc \cos A$

$$\cos A = \frac{b^2 + c^2 - a^2}{2bc}$$

Area of triangle $= \frac{1}{2} ab \sin C$

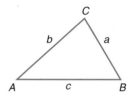

The quadratic equation

The solutions of $ax^2 + bx + c = 0$, where $a \neq 0$, are given by

$$x = \frac{-b \pm \sqrt{b^2 - 4ac}}{2a}$$

Standard deviation

Standard deviation for a set of numbers $x_1, x_2, \ldots, x_n$, having a mean of $\bar{x}$, is given by

$$s = \sqrt{\frac{\sum(x - \bar{x})^2}{n}} \quad \text{or} \quad s = \sqrt{\frac{\sum x^2}{n} - \left\{\frac{\sum x}{n}\right\}^2}$$

Answers

Number and algebra

Place value and the number system

1. (a) 2.98 (b) 4000
2. (a) 2 (b) −6 (c) −30
   (d) 4 (e) −8 (f) −10
3. −2.1625
4. π, $\sqrt{3}$, $(\sqrt{5} - 1)$, $(\sqrt{5} - 1)^2$
5. $\dfrac{217}{999}$
6. (a) a^6 (b) b^{-1} or $\dfrac{1}{b}$
7. $n = 3$
8. (a) 4.61×10^8 (b) 7.2×10^{-5}
9. (a) 363 000 (b) 0.000 009 6
10. 2.21×10^{15}

Relationships between numbers and computation methods

1. (a) 41, 43, 47, 53, 59
   (b) $2^3 \times 5^2 \times 7$
   (c) (i) 70
       (ii) $2^3 \times 3^3 \times 5^2 \times 7^2 = 264\ 600$
2. (a) $1\frac{11}{36}$ (b) $1\frac{1}{3}$
3. $\dfrac{x - 3}{3x - 2}$
4. (a) $\frac{3}{8}$ (b) 599.2
5. 3700
6. (a) 3.04 (b) $\dfrac{16 + 14}{\sqrt{100}} = \dfrac{30}{10} = 3$
7. (a) upper bound = 12.85 cm
       lower bound = 12.75 cm

(b)   upper bound = 51.4 cm

lower bound = 51.0 cm

(c)   upper bound = 165.1225 cm^2

lower bound = 162.5625 cm^2

Solving numerical problems

1   (a)   3 : 4   (b)   15 : 1

(c)   2 : 125   (d)   3 : 4

2   (a)   A £250, B £187.50, C £62.50

(b) $\dfrac{90x}{3x}$ = 30; 30(x − 5) = 210, giving x = 12

3   Graph C. A straight line through (0, 0)

4   300

5   (a)   2.4 × 10^{19} (b)   5.38 × 10^{15}

6   $\dfrac{8.45 \times 3.65 - 8.35 \times 3.55}{8.35 \times 3.55}$ × 100%

= 4.05% (correct to 3 s.f.)

Functional relationships

1   (a)   21 000 cm^3

(b)   2930 cm^2

2   (a)   7, 9, 11 and 13

(b)   All second differences = 2

(c) $u_n = (n + 2)^2 - 3$ or $(n + 1)^2 + 2n$

Both simplify to $u_n = n^2 + 4n + 1$

3   (a) $y = -\dfrac{3}{2}x + 4$

(b)   gradient $= -\dfrac{3}{2}$

4

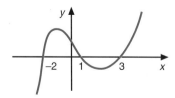

5   $a \approx 1.4$, $b \approx 3.8$

6   $y = (x - 5)^2 + 4$

Equations and formulae

1　(a)　$6x^2 - 6x + 1$

　　(b)　$\dfrac{5x}{3y^2}$

2　(a)　$x^2 - 11x + 14$

　　(b)　$8xy^3(2x + 3z)$

　　(c)　$(x + y)(x - y)$

　　(d)　$(4p + 9q)(4p - 9q)$

3　$T = 4ml^2n^2$

4　$x > -1$

5　$x = 3, y = -2$

6　(a)　$(x + 7)(x - 5)$

　　(b)　$x = -7$ or $x = 5$

　　(c)

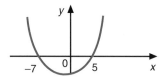

　　(d)　$-7 < x < 5$

7　(a)　$x = 6.19$ or $x = 0.807$ (to 3 s.f.)

　　(b)　$0.807 < x < 6.19$

8　$2^3 - 2 \times 2 = 4$　　　(< 19)

　　$3^3 - 2 \times 3 = 21$　　　(> 19)

　　$x = 2.92$

Shape, space and measures
Properties of shapes

1　$x = 6.8$ cm, $\theta = 53°$

2　20

3　$x = 60°, y = 110°$

4　$x = 5.55$ m, $y = 6.42$ m, area $\Delta BCD = 16.1$ m^2

5　(a)　60° or 120°

　　(b)　135° or 225°

6

$$y = 1 + \sin 2x$$

91

Properties of position, movement and transformation

1   (a) $\vec{AC} = 3\mathbf{a} + 3\mathbf{b}$, $\vec{PQ} = 2\mathbf{a} + 2\mathbf{b}$

    (b) Parallel

2

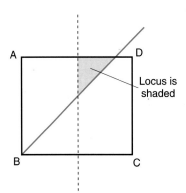

Locus is shaded

3

   (a) (i) Reflection in $x = \frac{1}{2}$

       (ii) $180°$ rotation about $(\frac{1}{2}, -\frac{1}{2})$

   (b) $(-1, -3)$

   (c) Check translated image.

4   1620 kg

5   (a) 115 km   (b) 328.6°

Measures

1   $15 \times 4.5 = 67.5$; closest is 70 l

2   1040 kg/m^3 (correct to 3 s.f.)

3   (a) 13.4 cm (3 s.f.)

   (b) 47.0 cm^2 (3 s.f.)

   (c) 24.0 cm^2 (3 s.f.)

4   Perimeter $= \sqrt{x^2 + 2yz}$

   Area $= \dfrac{\pi(x^3 + y^3)}{x + 2y + 3z}$

   Volume $= \dfrac{x^3 + x^2y + 5yz^2}{11\sqrt{2}}$

Handling data

Processing and interpreting data

1 Stratified sampling is more appropriate in any situation where the population is divided into groups that should be represented in proportion to their size.

2 (a) Check frequency polygons.

(b) mean (first) = 34;

mean (last) = 28

(c) The mean number of merits per pupil is significantly less in the last half-term and this change is also shown by the shift in the modal class. The general downward trend is not so evident at the top end of the scale, i.e. among those with the highest number of merits.

3 The interquartile range is not affected by extreme values in the same way as the range.

4 (a) mean = 14.3

standard deviation = 2.62

(b) The mean value is increased by n, but the standard deviation is unchanged.

(c) mean = 15.1

standard deviation = 2.62

Estimating and calculating the probabilities of events

1 (a) $P(A \text{ or } C) = \frac{19}{20}$

(b) $P(A) + P(B) > 1$ so A and B cannot be mutually exclusive.

(c) $P(A) \times P(B) = \frac{3}{4} \times \frac{2}{3} = \frac{1}{2}$

$\quad\quad = P(A \text{ and } B)$

so A and B are independent.

2 Check tree diagram.

(a) $\frac{5}{36} + \frac{5}{36} = \frac{5}{18}$

(b) $\left(\frac{5}{6}\right)^3 = \frac{125}{216}$

(c) $1 - \frac{125}{216} = \frac{91}{216}$

3 (a) $\dfrac{7}{102}$ (b) $\dfrac{21}{102}$

(c) $\dfrac{18}{18 + 56} = \dfrac{9}{37}$

4 (a) $\dfrac{4}{216} = \dfrac{1}{54}$

(b) $(500 \times £0.50) - (500 \times \frac{1}{54} \times £10)$

$= £157$ (to the nearest £1)

Index

This page can be used for your own notes